TURNING TABLES

Six Lessons You Need to Unlearn

Steve McVey

TWS | THE WRITER'S SOCIETY PUBLISHING

Published in the United States of America

Paperback: ISBN 978-1-961180-44-4

TWS Publishing
Lodi, CA
www.thewriterssociety.online

CONTENTS

INTRODUCTION
TABLES OF TRADITION

*There are more things in heaven and earth, Horatio,
than are dreamt of in your philosophy" – Hamlet*

I grew up under a steeple, attending church every Sunday since before first grade. My parents had a sincere faith, which they passed on to me. I was surrounded and anchored by a caring community of friends, teachers, and pastors who cultivated my spiritual roots.

At the young age of nineteen, I became the senior pastor of a loving congregation of people who were gentle and nurturing in ways that helped me grow in wisdom and experience. I served as a senior pastor in various churches for over two decades and was sincere at every step of the way.

Yet, having been connected to that community as both a church member and a pastor for most of my life, I discovered something amiss. Some of the things I was taught in church and consequently taught others as a pastor are radically different from what I've come to know since stepping back, opening my mind, and taking a fresh look at what I'd been told and then taught.

Some of what we've been taught to be true has been diluted. A diluted truth becomes a polluted truth, which is no truth at all. Jesus said, "A little leaven leavens the whole lump." That is what has happened with the topics considered in this book. *Turning Tables* considers six topics that have been distorted over time and have been detrimental to many.

Chapter one sets the tone for the book by pressing the reset button in the reader's mind in showing that love isn't just something God does. It's who He is. That statement may sound simple but most people don't get it. They still think that love is one of the attributes of God, not realizing that it is His very nature and that everything about Him must be understood through that lens.

The second chapter tackles the subject of divine justice by showing the tension between God's justice and man's justice. Seeing the contrast between the justice of jurisprudence and the justice of Jesus will forever change your mind about how the rule of God works in this life.

Chapter three goes straight to the fires of hell by taking an ancient look at the meaning of God's wrath. Will God's patience one day be exhausted and He will then morph into a vengeful, punishing deity who will pay people back for doing wrong and rejecting Him? That's what we've often been told but nothing could be further from the truth. This chapter will offer and prove a different way of seeing this subject.

The last three chapters speak to the way we see ourselves. Chapter four goes straight to the heart of our identity by challenging what we've been told about being just a "sinner saved by grace." When you see the truth that actually disproves that statement, you'll discover that the old way of seeing this issue will debilitate anybody who believes it.

Chapter five tackles the whole problem of the emphasis on morality in the modern church. Sin-management may well be the most problematic protocol of modern ministry. You'll finish this chapter by deciding to never again promise God you'll try harder to do better. There is a better way than moral living. It's miraculous living and this chapter will lead you to that lifestyle.

The final chapter comes to a crescendo by leading readers to abandon shame and accept the reality that sin has been fully dealt with and is *gone*. Having counseled many ridden with guilt for fifty years, I can attest that it is, by far, the most debilitating problem that affects people, especially those who've been indoctrinated by legalistic religion.

The subject matter of these six topics is consistently being told and sold in the modern world of Christendom. It's important to remember that just because we've heard some-thing a thousand times doesn't make it true. Well-meaning but misguided teachers may have misled you. That's as much a confession as a critique. I did it for decades and acknowledge that. Then I changed (repented) and, if needed, I hope you will too. Don't take my word for what I present in this book, but don't take theirs either. I've given ample biblical and historical evidence here. Search it out for yourself.

This gap between popular religious beliefs and actual spiritual reality isn't new. It's what prompted Jesus to over-turn tables of tradition in His earthly lifetime, both figuratively and literally. His revolution of grace aimed to unveil some things people had been misinformed about in church (synagogue) or else not heard of at all. To do that, He had to challenge existing beliefs. His message and ministry were contrarian to religious culture in many ways. He told them about things they had gotten wrong and some they had never even considered. In short, He was a disruptor of the religious system.

My goal in this book is similar. The intent here isn't to be condescending or insulting to those doing their best with the information they've been given. As an insider, I know that space well. I spent decades with my heart in the right place while my head was in the wrong place. My aim here isn't to throw stones but to stimulate thinking. What if there are truths about God that many of us have yet to grasp? What if some of what we've been told is wrong? What if changing beliefs in a few key areas could transform your life for the better? Would you be open to that, even if it meant casting off old viewpoints and accepting new ones?

Are you willing to have your tables of
tradition that have misrepresented

the truth to be overturned? What
if we need to change how we see
God to know Him truthfully?
What if we even need to change
how we see ourselves and that
we're not who we've been told
we are?

Maybe there are some tables of tradition that need to be overturned in your belief system. Let's get real for a moment: What are the chances that you ended up in the exact place where you were taught the truth, the whole truth, and nothing but the truth? You are one of the fortunate few to get it exactly right. C'mon. The very idea reeks with pride, doesn't it? Of course, we aren't right about everything we believe. Some things are on target, and other things need to be challenged. That's why questioning is essential. Some of what we've thought of as sacred doctrines are actually sacred cows that need to be put down.

You may need to get it out of your mind that doubt about things you've believed is a bad thing. God doesn't mind if we carefully question and think more deeply, even about the long-held beliefs we learned at home and in church. He crafted our brains for continued growth toward maturity in understanding. We don't need to be afraid of losing our faith by asking honest questions or reexamining our assumptions. If our faith is that fragile, we're probably headed for trouble anyway.

The Spirit Jesus promised would teach us often initially unsettles us to lead us into fuller understanding. People are sometimes afraid of being misled when they hear something new to them, but Jesus warned about a different danger when He spoke of "invalidating the word of God by your tradition which you have handed down" (Mark 7:13, NASB). The risk of missing the truth by unquestioningly believing what we've been told is real. Some of what we've been taught as sound theology is nothing more than a religious philosophy that needs to be reexamined. It has been rightly said that it's as important to have questions about answers as it is to have answers to questions.

Questioning what we've been told is fundamental to spiritual growth and personal development. It involves a journey from accepting information at face value to engaging critically with ideas, promoting a deeper understanding of who God is, who we are, and what life is meant to be. This process of inquiry challenges us to examine our beliefs, confront biases, discover blind spots, and consider perspectives different from our own. Through this questioning, we develop the ability to think independently of what we've been told, relying on the Spirit to help us make informed decisions and cultivate a deeper sense of authentic faith. Additionally, questioning encourages a lifelong pursuit of knowledge and truth, continually guiding us to grow and adapt our understanding based on greater insight. In essence, questioning enriches our grace walk by empowering us to keep growing and learning in a healthy progression.

I invite you to join me in the following chapters as we explore significant areas where our viewpoints may require expansion, revision, or even replacement. Some ideas may surprise or even disturb you, just as Jesus' first followers felt uncomfortable when He challenged the religious norms of His day. But let's approach this journey with an open yet discerning mindset, willing to follow Truth and trust God to reshape our thinking where needed. It's a mature person who has learned not to immediately dismiss something that won't instantly fit inside a mental folder that already exists in her beliefs. Sometimes, we need to create new folders or discard specific files we've kept there. I'm not asking you to be gullible. I'm encouraging you to be teachable and to do the work by prayerfully searching these things out for yourself.

As we journey together through the upcoming chapters, I invite you to join me in an enlightening exploration of subjects that define us—God and ourselves. Who is God? Who are you? There are no more critical questions to answer in life.

I challenge you to approach these subjects with an open mind, ready to discover truths that might surpass what you've previously encountered in church. Let's move forward on this discovery with curiosity and a willingness to see these topics in a different, uplifting light. While there is no "new truth," there certainly is new understanding when we gain new information and revelation of the truth. Let's agree that the One Jesus promised would "guide you into all truth" will do that very thing as you read, even if it means turning tables over which have held your beliefs until now.

CHAPTER 1

FROM POMP TO PAPA

A NEW PERSPECTIVE ON GOD'S LOVE

God's love is like a light, filling every corner of the universe with its radiance. —*The Divine Comedy*

One time, when I was speaking in England, dear friends there gifted my wife and me a very special experience. Because of their connections, we were able to visit the House of Parliament and sit in the peanut gallery as members of the House of Lords debated national policy. It was a memorable experience highlighting our many visits to the United Kingdom.

After the robust debate ended, our experience became even better. We were ushered to a section of Parliament where the public wasn't allowed to visit. We stood in a corridor admiring the beauty of our surroundings when suddenly everybody came to attention, and we were asked to stand back against the wall. As we stepped back, a door opened, and out walked the Lord Chancellor, who moved past us, wearing his "full-bottomed wig," the white wig that is part of the formal attire worn in certain legal proceedings and ceremonies. I felt like I was in an 18th-century courthouse where barristers were about to argue their cases before a majestic magistrate. The sense of pomp and pageantry was palpable for this American. It was a special privilege to be able to see these sights, which are usually obscured from the public.

THE AUDACITY OF INTIMACY

Let me now move beyond what actually happened and ask you to use your imagination to illustrate a point. What if it had been Queen Elizabeth who had walked out? What if, at that moment, I had stepped forward and cheerfully blurted, "Hey, Liz! Great to see you! You're looking good. How's Chuck (Prince Charles)?" The very idea of such a thing is absurd. Only a fool would do such a disrespectful thing.

This example illustrates the problem first-century religionists had with the way Jesus referred to and talked about God. Because of the type of reverence they had for God, they often avoided using any name at all when they referred to Him. Jews still often use the word *Hashem* to avoid being disrespectful to the holy name of God. The word means "the name," and when they use it, everybody knows who they're talking about without having to say the name.

If Jewish people refer to God by name, they often use *Adonai*, which means "Lord." Sometimes, they use *Elohim*, the plural form, meaning "God." The four-letter "tetra-grammaton" is the most sacred name of God in Israel. When transliterated into English, it is spelled JHVH or YHWH. To pronounce it, one must add vowels, resulting in Jehovah or Yahweh.

From a Jewish perspective, the point is that God is exalted so far above lowly man that He should be regarded as such in the way He is referenced. This practice extends to writing as well, where God's names and even His title are often abbreviated (e.g., writing "G-d" instead of "God") to show respect and to ensure that the name is not defaced or used casually. Books and materials containing the name of God are treated with great respect. They aren't placed on the floor; if they fall, they are picked up immediately. When such texts become worn or are no longer usable, they are not simply thrown away but are buried in a Jewish cemetery or stored in a *genizah*, a repository for sacred texts awaiting burial.

REDEFINING REVERENCE

It was into that culture that Jesus came and disrupted their views about the nature of God. While we all recognize the rightfulness of a reverent attitude toward God, Jesus redefined what that means by shifting the perception from institutional respect to intimate relationship.

When Jesus dared to refer to God as *Abba*, the people were both shocked and outraged. How could He have the audacity to address the Creator and Sustainer of All Things by using a word small children would speak to their papa? They wouldn't even dare to utter God's holy name, yet Jesus called Him "Papa." No wonder this grace bomb shook their sense of sanctity to its foundation. Their religious, rigid minds indignantly convulsed seeing Jesus relate to the Eternal God with such familiarity.

> What they didn't get, but you and I do, is that He was trying to make a point. He wanted them to see God in a different way. To do that, Jesus refused to conform to their culture or fit into their formulas. Their view of God needed to change, and Jesus was willing to do what it took to cause them to see that need. He wanted them to know His Father in a deeper and more meaningful way and was willing to do whatever was necessary to help them.

He's still acting that way today. Now, as then, Jesus enters our modern self-satisfaction and challenges our limited mindsets. He peels back religious layers that hide the truths we need to understand to experience the life we were born to know and enjoy. In a way that isn't so different from first-century Jews, people today still have a short-sighted or even wrong concept of God.

Jesus still longs to make His Abba known to us. What if much we were taught fails to align with actual spiritual reality? Let's consider some things we've likely been told about God and hold them up to the mirror of truth found in Jesus Christ and the Bible.

The revelation of God in Jesus Christ uncovers a unique Triune essence, existing in a union of three distinct Persons who together make up the One. This is a starting place for understanding the nature of God. Some people dismiss the importance of the Trinity, but it is important for several reasons. Understanding the Trinity's significance goes beyond what many have been taught. The core question arises: Why is the triune aspect of God so important? Why does it matter so much?

The answer is that, above everything else, God is inherently centered in relationships. The Father, Son, and Holy Spirit have eternally existed in an intense bond of love, a perpetual and intimate union within the Trinity that has always and will always exist. To put it simply, God Himself is a community of love.

The Apostle John said it clearer than anybody when he wrote, "God is love" (1 John 4:7-8). This simple yet profound statement encapsulates the essence of who God is. When we contemplate God, we essentially contemplate a Being defined by reciprocal love. Not understanding this leads to a distorted, damaging, and misguided perception of Him. Grasping the concept of this heavenly "Circle of Love'" might be the most critical aspect of understanding the nature of God.

This characteristic of God's nature is necessary because it unveils the relational aspect of the Divine. The Bible begins with the words, "In the beginning God . . ." The Hebrew word used there for God is *Elohim*, the plural name previously mentioned. The first thing the Bible implies about God by using that name is that He is relational.

Consider this: if God's triune, communal nature is the first thing He reveals in Scripture, doesn't it underscore its importance in how we see and understand Him? God is not a solitary entity but a triune engaged in profound, intimate interactions within the Trinity. It's a Circle of Love, Laughter, and Life. This understanding can shape our relationship with Him by emphasizing a God who isn't just a distant deity who directs this world but a dedicated Dad who is deeply devoted to us inside an intimate relationship.

This triune nature speaks volumes about the high value of relationships in the divine order of things and suggests that at the heart of all existence is a fundamental interconnect-edness. It also invites and empowers us to express this Reality in our lives, promoting a life defined by loving rela-tionships. Understanding the Trinity this way becomes a pathway to understanding the nature of Ultimate Reality and our place in it.

The nature of God's love stands independent of our actions or reactions. No matter what happens in this world, God is love. This fundamental attribute of God needs to be the foundation of our understanding of His entire being. Think about it this way: Is love simply an attribute of God, or does John's affirmation highlight the very essence of His identity? Should we consider other aspects of His nature alongside His love? The unequivocal answer is that love isn't just a part of who God is but the fabric of His being.

Consider this: when we insist, 'Yes, God is loving, but He is also just!' aren't we inadvertently pouring water into wine, diluting the essence of God's love? Picture God's justice not as a stern judge with a gavel but as a skilled gardener, care-fully pruning a treasured vine. Just as pruning is necessary for the vine to grow and be fruitful, God's justice, inter-twined with His love, isn't about punishment but nurturing growth. Can you see how, in God's hands, justice and love are not two separate forces but one seamless garment woven with threads of mercy, grace, and restoration? The next chapter will reveal a divine justice that looks like that.

To be properly understood, everything has to be filtered through
God's love. God has no attributes
that stand in contrast to love
because He is love and will never
act out of character. Love is more
than an attribute of God. It is
who He is.

To respond to a pure expression of God's love with a caveat about His holiness as if the two aren't in synch misrepresents Him. What does it mean to say that God is holy? God's holiness doesn't suggest that His purity insulates Him inside a sterile environment that can't tolerate the presence of sinful germs. That viewpoint leaves people with the idea that the most important thing to Him about us is that we behave morally. Whatever you do, be sure to avoid sins because He can't abide that. We'll say more about sin in another chapter, but for now, let's be clear: God loved us so much that He threw Himself into the cesspool of sin to rescue us from it. That is the essence of the incarnation.

God stepped into time and space in the person of Jesus Christ and became a man to deal with the issue of sin face-to-face. Get it out of your head that God shirks back from sin. He does not. The birth of Jesus proves that.

Rethinking Sin's Effect on God

The origin of the belief that God can't be anywhere near sin finds its roots at the very beginning – in the Garden of Eden. This cancerous idea first infected Adam when, having sinned, he felt the need to hide from God. He wrongly assumed that his sin made him unworthy of being in God's presence. He thought God couldn't tolerate a person who had disobeyed Him. This first instance of somebody thinking God couldn't handle the fact that he sinned set the stage for a misconception about God's relationship with man and his sin that still affects people today. Adam thought God would be put off by His sin, but He was wrong. God came looking for Adam after he sinned.

This wrong belief that Adam had about God's relationship to sin has been passed down from generation to generation. By the time we reach the prophets of the Old Testament, it is clear that this wrong concept of God has diseased the whole human race. Habakkuk 1:13 describes the prophet's thoughts on the subject. He was seriously distressed by the wrong he saw being done to Israel, so he brought his faulty viewpoint to God in prayer: "Your eyes are too pure to look upon evil. You cannot tolerate wrongdoing" (NIV). There, Habakkuk expressed the same viewpoint Adam had held. God can't look upon sin. There it is, right in the Bible, but there's more to understand that will clarify the matter.

Habakkuk's expression shows his struggle to understand God's attitude about sin. It highlights a common problem that still affects how people see God. It happens when we use the wrong lens to read the Bible. A proper study of the Bible plainly shows that God's nature is not to shun sinners but to seek them out, just as He demonstrated with Adam after the fall. Contrary to the idea of a god who distances Himself from sin, Adam's story shows that God rushes toward those who are infected by sin.

If we were to come to our decision about God and sin based on what Habakkuk said about God not being able to look upon evil, it would seem evident that God can't bear the sight of sin. This interpretation is the one many people still hold today. It comes from an approach to the Bible that often leads to saying, "The Bible plainly says it, so I believe it." This approach oversimplifies how we interpret Scripture. We get into trouble when we take parts of Scripture out of context, and sadly, people often do that. My book, *Unlock Your Bible*, speaks in depth about how to read and understand the Bible. A flat reading of Scripture happens when we read and interpret the Old and New Testament in the same way. That is not how the Bible is intended to be understood, and it causes problems when we do that.

Have you ever thought that the God of the New Testament looks different from the Old Testament? There's a reason it seems that way, and an answer to that dilemma comes from knowledge of "hermeneutics," which is the science of biblical interpretation. If you have questions about this subject, I recommend you get my book, *Unlock Your Bible*. The book will help you understand the different approaches we are to take to the Old and New Testaments. I also have a teaching series on the subject that you can watch on my YouTube channel.

People have used Habakkuk's words for centuries to "prove" that God can't look upon sin. The tragic thing is that to do that, they have to ignore the rest of the verse. Habakkuk continues in his prayer, "Your eyes are too pure to look on evil; you cannot tolerate wrongdoing. Why, then, do you tolerate the treacherous? Why are you silent while the wicked swallow up those more righteous than themselves?"

Do you see his problem? He argues that God can't look upon evil and questions, "Why then do you?" How God behaved didn't align with what Habakkuk thought about Him. His theology was wrong. Thankfully, God's love is bigger than our wrong ideas about Him. He doesn't jump back from our wrongdoing but jumps into our mess and stands with us, leading us forward into wholeness.

The stories of Adam's cringing and Habakkuk's crying point toward the view that the majority in the modern church still holds. It's the idea that the most important thing to God is that we avoid sin. What a horrible lie! It has led people to have the mindset that morality is what is most important. Do right and avoid wrong. It has led the church to engage in the sin-management business by making eradicating sin the focal point of its mission. It has led to a religious life sentence in which many sincere people can't take their eyes off themselves and their behavior and put their eyes on Jesus Christ, where they belong. It has led to a contamination of what we call "the gospel" by starting with humanity's problem of sin instead of beginning with God's love for humanity. It has led sincere believers to try to live a moral lifestyle and blinded them to the potential of a miraculous lifestyle.

The antidote to sin isn't morality. The cure for sin is Jesus Christ. "Look and live!" Moses told the children of Israel in the wilderness when venomous snakes poisoned them. It was by looking at the bronze serpent mounted on a pole and lifted up (a foreshadowing of what Jesus would do) that they would find healing. The principle hasn't changed. Only when people look to the One lifted up on the cross will they find healing. There is no other way. If you are going to have a clearer picture of who God is, it's essential to stop smearing His face with the mud of morality, seeing Him as a conduct cop who is more interested in your behavior than anything else. No, God's greatest interest is you and your welfare. The relevance of sin is directly proportionate to how it hurts you, not God.

> Spiritual growth requires that we abandon any viewpoint that suggests that God relates to sin as Superman would relate to kryptonite. God's only concern with sin is what it does to you. It has

nothing to do with morals that
find their roots in the Tree of the
Knowledge of Good and Evil – a
tree God instructed humanity to
avoid.

Adam got it wrong. Habakkuk got it wrong. Have you
gotten it wrong? Renowned Scottish author George
MacDonald rightly said, "Good souls, many will one day be
horrified at the things they now believe of God." Believing
that God distances Himself from people because of sin is a
horrifying prospect. It has caused many to think they are
"away from the Lord" when they misbehave. Nothing could
be further from the truth. He will never leave or forsake you.
Never.

The interpretation of Habakkuk's misguided prayer invites
us to reevaluate what we've believed about God's holiness
and His relationship with sin. It challenges us to consider a
God who is not only transcendent in purity but also imma-
nently involved with a fallen world that needs healing.

Don't you love that God's grace is bigger than our
misconceptions? He is good whether we believe or even
know it or not. God didn't act like Habakkuk thought He
should. Thankfully, He still doesn't always act like we think
He should today. His nature is to love, and that is what He
does. Of course, God can look upon sin. Otherwise, how
would He have ever looked at the people He had created?

Sin doesn't scare God. That's why Jesus came to this world —
to defeat it and put it away once and for all.

Positioning qualities like holiness and justice as separate but
equal to God's love distorts His true essence. That isn't to
suggest that these qualities are less than but are inside
Divine Love. Consider this analogy: If God's essence were
represented as a pie, how would you illustrate the relationship between His love, justice, and holiness? Would it be
appropriate to divide the pie into three equal segments, each
symbolizing a different aspect of His nature? Or would it be
more accurate to represent His love as the larger portion,
with justice and holiness as smaller segments? This analogy
will mislead us about the true nature of God.

In reality, dividing God's nature into distinct segments is
flawed. A more fitting representation would be to consider
God's love as the crust of the pie, encompassing and holding
together all His attributes. Whether it's His justice, holiness,
or even wrath, each must be interpreted as an extension of
His love. This perspective challenges the notion of God
being partly loving and partly other things, affirming instead
that every aspect of God emanates from and is enveloped in
His foundational nature of love.

Imagine being handed a glass of water, described as pure.
Naturally, you would assume the glass contains nothing but
water. If even the slightest impurity were present, calling it
"pure water" would be misleading. To use a crass example,

if somebody spits in a gallon of fresh water, you wouldn't drink it. That's a good illustration of what has happened in the modern church world. Because some don't understand that love is the defining essence of who God is, they have "spit" into the purity of His love by suggesting that other things contradicting love are equally a part of who He is.

Consider the implications if God were partly loving but also possessed characteristics that conflicted with love, as some believe. How could we be sure that we wouldn't encounter an aspect of God that is less than loving? Or even one that is the opposite of love? This kind of doubt would disrupt our peace and confidence in our relationship with Him. Imagine a deity dispensing something other than love – a concept more aligned with Freddy Krueger (the horror film character) than Jesus Christ.

AN UNSHAKABLE FOUNDATION

A transformation in my life happened when I came to the unwavering realization that God is love. I interpret everything, even the Bible, through that realization. If it doesn't look like Love, either the evidence is incomplete or (like Haggai) my understanding of the evidence is wrong. Before embracing the Christ-grounded perspective, my faith in His unchanging love was sometimes threatened. Various triggers would cause me to question and doubt: challenging life circumstances, confusing Old Testament verses, or even witnessing global events in the news that seemed inconsistent with a God of pure love. Many things made me wonder at times.

The significant shift happened when I focused on Jesus Christ as the manifestation of God. The Bible describes Him as the "exact expression of His (Father's) being" (Hebrews 1:3). If this is true, we must ask, "Did Jesus leave out any part of His Father's nature?" Was there something He chose not to tell us?

> The prospect that Jesus might have hidden a "darker side" of the Father while assuring us that "Anyone who has seen Me has seen the Father" (John 14:9) raises serious concerns. Wouldn't an omission like this not be deceptive? But this isn't the case.

We can be assured there is no hidden part of God that Jesus failed to reveal. You get the whole picture in Jesus Christ, not a sanitized version of God.

The realization that God's nature is pure love changes everything. It allows us to interpret the world, the Bible, and our personal experiences through the lens of this unshakeable truth. Every characteristic of God, whether it's His justice, holiness, or even wrath, must be understood in light of His fundamental essence of love. This understanding brings coherence to our understanding of His attributes, causing us to see how they all fit together. It offers an unshakable foundation for our faith that allows us to relax and enjoy.

Make Jesus the sole guide in your attempt to understand the Father. The Bible tells us, "In the past, God spoke to our ancestors through the prophets at many times and in various ways, but in these last days, he has spoken to us by his Son" (Hebrews 1:1- 2). It is through Jesus that the Father's true nature is revealed, and what Jesus indisputably shows us is that the essence of the Father is Love – pure and simple. If it doesn't look like Jesus, it's not God.

Stop lifting out Old Testament verses that seem to suggest a dark side to God, and let Jesus be the lens you use to see who the Father is. There certainly are subjects we've been taught in church that seem to stand in contrast to His love, but if you were told that God is more than love, you've been told something wrong. Nothing about God contradicts His love. It would help if you settled this matter in your mind. Is God pure love or not? Is love just one aspect of His nature, but others contradict love? How you answer this will not only determine how you see Him but also affect how you see everything.

The revelation that the core of God's nature is love isn't just a theological truth; it's a practical truth that will transform your life. It shapes our relationship with Him, our understanding of the world, and our interactions with others. Seeing the Trinity as a never-ending circle of love reveals our place and connection within God's plan. Embracing this perspective deepens our sense of connection with God, uplifts our lives, and enriches our grace walk in profound ways.

QUESTIONS FOR REFLECTION

1. How does the author's portrayal of God as "Papa" instead of a distant, judgmental figure challenge your existing beliefs about God's nature?
2. Discuss the significance of understanding God's love as His essence rather than just one of His attributes. How does this shift in perspective affect your relationship with Him?
3. Reflect on the metaphor of God's love being like sunlight that nourishes or scorches, depending on one's reception. How do you personally experience God's love in your life?
4. In what ways have traditional religious teachings complicated your understanding of God's love, and how does this book propose to simplify that understanding?
5. The author suggests a journey from seeing God through the lens of fear to experiencing His love as freedom. Share a personal experience that echoes this transition.

CHAPTER 2

FROM REVENGE TO RESTORATION

A NEW PERSPECTIVE ON GOD'S JUSTICE

It is justice, not vengeance, that is the
true value of humanity. - Rumi

Any conversation about God's nature frequently ignites discussions about divine justice, a topic that often leads to an imagined dichotomy between His inherent love and His sense of justice. This contrast arises because these two are commonly viewed as separate or conflicting facets of God's character.

In the last chapter, we discussed how having a proper concept of God necessitates seeing every aspect of Him through the lens of His love. To grasp a true and accurate understanding, it usually becomes imperative to reevaluate the meaning of His justice.

Misinterpretations of this subject have led to widespread confusion about how to reconcile the image of a merciful, loving God with one who also appears to punish without compassion. This confusion stems from the misguided conception of a god who, in reality, doesn't even exist. The God Jesus came to reveal is nothing like the god many have created in their minds due to a wrong understanding of what divine justice is.

The common insistence that "Yes, God is loving, but He is also just!" dilutes the essence of God's love by separating love and justice. God is more than loving. He is love, and as such, His execution of justice in no way contradicts His nature. It's easy to see how, on the surface, love and justice might appear contradictory. This flawed perspective inadvertently taints God's character by insinuating that when it comes to divine justice, love has to be temporarily suspended for justice to be carried out. If we are ever to be free from this misunderstanding, we must revisit and dig deeper into the true meaning of this topic.

The prevalent interpretation of "justice" often presents a picture of God that starkly contrasts with the way He is revealed through Jesus Christ for one main reason: It's because human justice is different from divine justice. The modern understanding of justice doesn't find its roots in the teachings of Jesus but in the tenets of legal jurisprudence.

Is it possible that our modern lens of justice, tinted by legalistic frameworks, blurs our vision of God's true nature? What if we viewed justice not as an unyielding scale, balancing rights and wrongs, but as a river, flowing with grace and mercy, finding ways to heal, cleanse, and renew people? Where a judicial approach usually punishes and segregates, divine justice, as Jesus exemplified, aims to embrace and transform. Can you see how justice then wouldn't be seen as a barrier but a bridge that connects, heals, and restores?

THE ORIGIN OF OUR UNDERSTANDING OF JUSTICE

The retributive view of justice forms the bedrock of the American legal system. It can be traced back to ancient Athens, six centuries before Christ. It is a system shaped significantly by Solon, known for his roles as a statesman, poet, and philosopher. Solon's era was a time of considerable transformation as society began to move away from the prevailing culture of retaliation that had long framed their civilization. He laid the groundwork for a democratic justice system by writing constitutions that introduced a public court system and involved juries composed of peers, a prosecutor, and a defense lawyer. The process took place under the oversight of a judge. Does this sound familiar? It should be because this Athenian model of justice governs judicial systems across the Western world, including the United States.[1]

Most of us believe it's a sound system for the courtrooms of society. Your understanding of justice probably comes from this historical context. It works well there, but here's an important thing to understand: This historical meaning of human justice is very different from the biblical portrayal of divine justice. God is not a courtroom judge. He is our Abba. Justice coming from Jesus is different from the justice coming from jurisprudence. God's justice is different from human justice, and that difference means everything to us. He's not into retribution but restoration.

> The concept of divine justice, as Jesus presented it in His teachings, is pivotal for our understanding of God. While human justice usually focuses on retribution, God's justice centers on restoration and reconciliation. Although courtrooms are into paying back those who did wrong, Christ is into putting back both for the one who was wronged and the one who did wrong. His goal is to restore everybody involved in the situation.

Jesus exemplified a vision of justice that transcends the pursuit of vengeance. Instead, it focuses on healing broken relationships and restoring what has been lost. This approach challenges the conventional view that justice necessitates punishment or retribution. On the contrary, it offers a perspective where justice becomes a conduit for healing, renewal, and restoration.

If we are to comprehend God's nature the way it was revealed through Jesus, we must recognize this crucial distinction. If we interpret divine justice through the lens of modern legal systems, we risk misrepresenting the true character of God as manifested in Christ. It's vital to differentiate between the legalistic concepts of human justice and the divine justice Jesus demonstrated. God's justice is rooted in love, not laws, and is oriented towards restoring harmony and peace.

Desmond Tutu, known for championing opposition to apartheid in South Africa, said, "The aim of justice is to repair a harm done, not to inflict another in return." That is the Christlike template of justice.

The conventional idea that wrongdoing requires punishment to settle the problem is deeply ingrained in our understanding. When we apply this template to God, there is no other way to see Him than as a stern courtroom Judge, handing out verdicts and sentences based on a strict sense of fairness. This perspective leads us to the belief that the consequences of sin have to be punished by God. It's no wonder so many see Him that way! We've wrongly put a

mask from the courtroom judges of this world on the face of
our Loving Abba!

> However, God's heart is not like that.
> He is fundamentally oriented
> towards restoration and reconcili-
> ation, not retribution. God isn't
> into payback. Don't punish it, but
> fix it. To him, it's not about
> revenge but restoration! God loves
> not only the offended but also the
> offender.

Divine justice is born from a unilateral love that doesn't
depend on what we do. "If we are faithless, he remains
faithful— for he cannot deny himself" (2 Timothy 2:13,
ESV). If God set aside love so that He could execute justice,
He would have to deny Himself, and that will never happen.
What, then, is the answer? The answer is that divine justice
isn't what most have been taught. Grace reaches out to
rescue and restore us because of His love. That's the kind of
justice He practices.

WHAT DOES THE BIBLE SAY?

Consider the profound message in Isaiah: 'Yet the Lord
longs to be gracious to you; therefore, he will rise up to show
you compassion. For the Lord is a God of justice. Blessed
are all who wait for him!' (Isaiah 30:18 NIV). What does this

verse say God desires? He yearns to extend grace and compassion. And why? Because "the Lord is a God of justice." His justice is rooted in love, not anger. This is the justice of agape — a justice that seeks to heal and restore rather than hurt and retaliate.

This grace-based, restorative justice is echoed in other biblical texts:

"Administer true justice; show mercy and compassion to one another" (Zechariah 7:9 NIV). How are we to administer true justice? By showing mercy and compassion.

"Learn to do right; seek justice. Defend the oppressed. Take up the cause of the fatherless; plead the case of the widow" (Isaiah 1:17 NIV). What does it look like to do right by seeking justice? It happens when we defend the oppressed and help the orphans and widows.

"Administer justice every morning; rescue from the hand of his oppressor the one who has been robbed" (Jeremiah 21:12 NIV). Justice focuses on rescuing from evil, not repaying the evil.

These passages emphasize mercy, compassion, defense of the vulnerable, and rescue. They portray justice that comes from divine love- the justice Jesus Christ embodied and brought into the world. Do you see the sharp difference between human justice and God's justice?

The prophecy in Matthew describes the mission of Jesus: "Look well at my handpicked servant; I love him so much, take such delight in him. I've placed my Spirit on him; he'll decree justice to the nations. But he won't yell, won't raise his voice; there'll be no commotion in the streets. He won't walk over anyone's feelings, won't push you into a corner. Before you know it, *his justice will triumph*" (Matthew 12:18-21 MSG, emphasis added).

This portrayal of justice, gentle yet triumphant, invites us to reconsider our understanding of divine justice and how we show justice to those who hurt us. Rather than a retributive framework, Godly justice is about elevating and rectifying what is wrong. It's a justice that uplifts rather than condemns. Eleanor Roosevelt rightly said, "Justice cannot be for one side alone, but must be for both." Divine justice isn't for one and against the other but is for everybody involved.

> This higher form of justice, grounded in grace and restoration, transforms our perception of God's nature and dealings with all of us. It reveals a God who is better than fair. He is faithful to lavish

His love, not seeking to punish but
to purify.

The Bible is filled with stories that illustrate the power of
divine justice. For instance, there's the story of Joseph in
Genesis 37-50. Joseph's brothers sold him into slavery out of
jealousy, and he eventually became a powerful figure in
Egypt. When his brothers came to Egypt seeking food
during a famine, Joseph had the opportunity to get revenge,
and nobody would have blamed him. Instead, he revealed
his identity, forgave his brothers, and invited them to live
with him. This act of forgiveness and reconciliation restored
the family and saved them from the famine. It was the just
thing to do.

It would be hard to find a person who hasn't heard the
parable of the prodigal son in Luke 15:11- 32. In this parable, a wayward son squanders his inheritance and returns
home expecting punishment. However, his father runs to
greet him with open arms, forgives him, and celebrates his
return. This story illustrates God's willingness to forgive and
restore without punishment. That's what divine justice looks
like.

Then there is the woman caught in adultery in John 8:1-11.
In this account, religious leaders brought a woman caught
in adultery to Jesus, seeking to have her stoned as the law
required. Instead of condemning her, Jesus challenged the
accusers, saying, "Let him who is without sin among you be

the first to throw a stone at her." The accusers dropped their stones and walked away, and Jesus told the woman to go and sin no more, offering her redemption and restoration instead of retribution. Mission accomplished. Justice was carried out.

Zacchaeus, the tax collector (Luke 19:1- 10), is another who comes to mind. He was a man known for his corruption, but he encountered Jesus and repented of his wrongdoing. He pledged to repay those he had cheated and to give generously to the poor. Jesus said, "Today salvation has come to this house," illustrating the transformative power of restorative justice.

The Apostle Peter's restoration in John 21:15-19 is further evidence. After denying Jesus three times, Peter experienced restorative justice when Jesus, after His resurrection, asked Peter three times if he loved Him. Peter's affirmation led to his reinstatement and commission to launch into ministry without guilt or shame.

These biblical examples are just a few that highlight the power of the kind of justice that offers forgiveness, reconciliation, and restoration. Human justice has its proper place in this world, but Jesus demonstrated how we can carry out holy justice in our relationships with others.

JESUS'S JUSTICE INSIDE OUR HUMAN HORRORS

Joe Avila's story is a poignant example of restorative justice in human relationships by reflecting the transformative power of forgiveness and redemption. One night, Joe, struggling with alcoholism, tragically caused the death of a young girl named Amy Wall in a drunk driving incident. Overwhelmed by guilt, he fled the scene but was later arrested. While in custody, Joe pursued a path not only to sobriety but to spiritual awakening.

Pleading guilty, Joe was sentenced to twelve years in prison.[2] There, he found purpose by serving in the prison's hospice. His journey in prison was not just about serving time; it was a transformative period of self-reflection and growth.

Upon his release, Joe was embraced by his community, especially the members of a local church. A significant moment in his journey occurred when he met Derek, Amy's brother, and later Rick Wall, her father. In an extraordinary display of grace, the Wall family, despite their unimaginable loss, had followed Joe's progress and offered him forgiveness. Rick's act of forgiving Joe, even before he asked for it, was a powerful testament to the healing potential of mercy and love.

Joe's transformation didn't stop at his release or the act of reconciliation. He dedicated his life to working tirelessly to support those incarcerated and their families. Inspired by the forgiveness and restoration he received, Joe's efforts in prison ministry have underscored the essence of restorative justice - it's not just about punishment, but rehabilitation, reconciliation, and the redemption of everybody involved. Miraculously, Joe and Amy's brother, Derek, would ultimately speak together at a Restorative Justice Council event. None, including Amy's family, would argue that Joe's incarceration was an inappropriate response from society, but her family didn't stop with societal justice alone but moved forward until they reached sacred justice. This kind isn't satisfied until redemption shows up on the scene.[3]

THE WAY WE VIEW GOD SHAPES OUR UNDERSTANDING OF JUSTICE

Our concept of God's justice fundamentally shapes how we relate to others. The lens through which we view Him — whether as a stern judge of strict punishment or as a source of boundless grace — significantly colors our actions and reactions in daily life. When we imagine Him as vindictive, we are likely to mirror that same trait, cultivating an eye-for-an-eye mentality that moves us further from understanding divine justice. On the other hand, understanding justice, as Jesus demonstrated, reframes our approach. This isn't just a theological stance; it's a transformative worldview that affects every interaction and decision we make.

In the authentic Christian culture,
divine justice is inseparable from
grace and mercy. This isn't a

balancing act where mercy coun-
terweighs justice. Instead, they are
seamlessly intertwined in the
fabric of God's character.

This Christlike union of justice and mercy becomes a gracious guide to us, leading us to offer compassion, understanding, and forgiveness, even when it's hard to do. It invites us to look beyond the surface of the wrong done to the deeper story of every individual.

Embracing the reality that God's justice encompasses restoration and redemption propels us toward reconciliation instead of retribution. It fosters a mindset where second chances aren't just possible but are a natural response to human failure. We begin to understand that everybody, including ourselves, is on a journey of growth and learning. This understanding nudges us to support the healing and growth of those who have made wrong choices, recognizing that punishment alone rarely leads to true transformation.

This perspective isn't about discarding justice in favor of mercy but redefining justice in a way that includes restoration. It's the Christ way. It motivates and empowers us to act justly, not out of a desire for revenge, but to bring about healing and wholeness. We are encouraged to love mercy, seeing it not as a weakness but as a formidable force that can break down barriers and heal hearts. And, in all of this, we are called to walk humbly, recognizing our potential to fall and the grace that has been extended to us.

This approach will significantly impact how we interact with those we encounter daily. It calls us to build relationships founded on grace and understanding, to listen empathetically, and to respond with patience. It's a journey towards creating a community where redemption isn't just a biblical topic but a way of life. We become architects of a space where every person feels valued, understood, and given the opportunity to rise above their past. That is what divine justice looks like!

In essence, our view of God's justice is a powerful tool that shapes us − not just our theological understandings but also our practical interactions. By adopting a Christ-centered view of justice and trusting Him to live through us, we express the unconditional love and forgiveness that God offers each of us. We create ripples of transformation in the world around us. In this space where justice and mercy meet, we truly reflect the heart of Christ Jesus, inviting others into a divine story of redemption and hope.

QUESTIONS FOR REFLECTION

1. How does the distinction between divine justice and human justice as presented in the book alter your view of how God deals with sin and sinners?

2. The concept of restorative justice is central to this chapter. Discuss a situation where you've witnessed or experienced justice that heals rather than punishes.

3. How does the author's interpretation of justice challenge conventional views of hell and divine punishment?

4. Reflect on the role of love in the administration of justice, both human and divine. Can you think of examples where love led to true justice?

5. How does understanding God's justice as a pursuit of restoration and reconciliation change the way you approach your own mistakes and those of others?

CHAPTER 3

FROM PUNISHMENT TO PASSION

A NEW PERSPECTIVE ON GOD'S WRATH

Who said anything about safe? 'Course he isn't safe. But he's good.
He's the King, I tell you. – The Lion, The Witch, and the Wardrobe

Any study of theology proper ultimately finds itself having to grapple with what the Bible teaches about the wrath of God. Few biblical concepts present such a profound paradox as how God's wrath can be reconciled with His love. The idea of "the wrath of God" typically conjures images of punishment and retribution—boils, pestilence, plagues, and captivity. You know—all those terrible things seen in the Old Testament.

Then comes Jesus to show us what the Father is like, and there is not one mention of payback by an angry God. If everything about the nature of God must be understood through Him, the personification of Divine Love, how can

we possibly make sense out of wrath? The answer lies in
how we define the word.[1]

While modern Evangelical thought associates the word with
a zealous expression of anger and retribution, we will
uncover how a more nuanced understanding of divine
wrath harmonizes with the irrefutable truth of God's nature
as love. By examining scriptural interpretations and the original linguistic distinctions of the word "wrath," we will
discover how what is often perceived as God's punitive
response is, in fact, an integral aspect of His profound love.
My goal in this chapter is not only to bridge the gap
between these two topics but to show how they are intrinsi-
cally interconnected, giving us an even clearer picture of the
God whose wrath in no way conflicts with His love.

Since Adam misjudged what God's response would be
immediately after the fall, people have projected onto Him
an angry disposition that does not exist toward us. What if
divine wrath isn't an expression of contemptuous anger but
an expression of God's love? The very idea challenges the
long-held beliefs of many, but you may discover it's not as
far-fetched an idea as you'd thought.

REDEFINING DIVINE WRATH

The linguistic roots of divine wrath offer valuable insight
into understanding divine wrath. The Apostle Paul, in
Romans 1:18- 19, introduces "wrath" using the original
language of the New Testament. The Greek word he used is

orgé. He wrote, "For the wrath (*orgé*) of God is revealed from heaven against all ungodliness and unrighteousness of men who suppress the truth in unrighteousness, because that which is known about God is evident within them; for God made it evident to them."

The New American Greek Lexicon offers two possible definitions of the word.[2] One definition focuses on anger, so the word certainly can mean that. However, there is also another possible meaning of the word. That meaning is defined as a movement or agitation of the soul caused by any strong emotion. The word's origin suggests reaching out with a quivering hand to grasp something one desires. This second definition is more about passion than anger. It's interesting to note that the word "orgé" is the root of the English words "orgasm" and "orgy." Clearly, those words have nothing to do with anger and everything to do with passion.

Think about how we use English words with varying meanings in everyday language. The same word can have different meanings based on how it is used. I might say, "I love my wife," or "I love my children," or "I love sushi," or "I love the old sixties rock n' roll music." What does the word "love" mean in those sentences? We can know for sure that the word will have a different definition in each of those statements. How do we know which meaning to apply? We know by context. Clearly, I don't love sushi the way I love my wife. Context identifies the difference in the meaning.

In the previous chapters, we've proven that God's nature is pure love. It's not just an attribute He possesses but defines His essence. It has been established that nothing but pure love could come from God; otherwise, His love couldn't truly be pure.

When determining the meaning of wrath in relationship to God, we must put the word into context. One meaning of the word denotes anger, and the other denotes the intense passion of any emotion, including love. Based on knowing that God's nature is pure love, which definition fits the context of His character? Will God one day tire of human foolishness, lose his patience, and unleash divine fury upon us? Or does it fit the context of who He is to suggest that the wrath of God has to do with a passionate love that refuses to give up on us? When we take a common-sense, informed approach to the issue, it becomes clear that His wrath is connected to His love and not a retributive anger that would contradict His very nature.

The wrath of God is His fierce love expressed with divine intensity and excitement. The noun "orgé" (ὀργή) has the same stem as the verb "orgáo" (ὀργάω), which generally means "I am eager" or "I am excited." God's excitement is toward people and against sin. He is eager to rescue us from it, not repay us for it.

Why, then, do so many believe that

God will one day run out of
patience, stop loving those who
don't love Him, and angrily
torment them, never to show any
mercy again? It's because they've
been brainwashed with a horren-
dous view of God. God's wrath is
not a time when the divine Dr.
Jekyll goes away and a ruthless
Mr. Hyde shows up on the scene.

Let what Jesus has revealed about the Father be your guide.
Was there ever a time when Jesus indicated that God is
vindictive toward those trapped in sin? Did He ever portray
God as a merciless courtroom judge who stands ready to
condemn sinners to suffer for it? Jesus portrayed God as a
Father who loves prodigals and receives them before they
even ask for forgiveness, as a Great Physician who came to
heal sinners, as a Shepherd who will stop at nothing to
rescue even one, and in many other ways that show His love.
Don't let brainwashing from sincere but misguided teaching
spoil your potential to revel in grace. God is for us, and
although He may feel anger toward the sin that can destroy
us, He never feels anger toward His precious children.

WHAT ABOUT HELL?

The subject of hell has come under scrutiny over the last
few years more than any other biblical topic I've seen
debated. Some have outright denounced the idea of hell's
existence because they have concluded that their only option

is to either believe in the kind of hell they were taught exists or else wholly reject it. I join those who reject the Augustinian version of infernalism many in the modern church world hold today.

Infernalism insists on a literal fire where God consciously torments people as His revenge against them for not receiving Him. The idea is that He loves them, but if they don't love Him back, He will one day stop loving them and will torment them forever to pay them back for not loving Him. It's not an exaggeration to say that this is the predominant view in today's Evangelical world. It posits a narcissistic god who "will show you" if you choose to disregard His love. That is not the Abba of Jesus. He does not tell us to love and forgive endlessly, while He won't do the same.

Others have embraced annihilationism, the belief that unbelievers will eventually be destroyed and cease to exist. I reject that viewpoint, too. We are spirits by nature, and even science has affirmed that energy can never be destroyed. It can mutate but not disintegrate. You will not die when your body does. You are a spirit being who will continue to live on.

It is essential to know that infernalism and annihilationism are not the only ways to interpret what the Bible says about hell. There is another way that is consistent with the nature of God and the human spirit.

It might be helpful to note that,
historically, the subject of hell has
never been considered a fundamental facet of the Christian
faith. We don't all have to agree
on this subject. We never have.

Even Augustine, the champion of eternal torment, wrote early in the fifth century, "There are very many who, though not denying the Holy Scriptures, do not believe in endless torments."[3]

That has changed over the past few years in some parts of the church world. Nowadays, you had better not only believe in hell but you'd better also believe it is what some say it is, or else be prepared to be called a heretic. As you consider this subject, please remind yourself that there have always been differences of opinion within the church about the nature of hell. A closed-minded posture about this subject doesn't honor Christ and shows scholastic shallowness in pursuing biblical truth. It's not compromising to take another look at what the Bible says to check our beliefs.

This closed mindset is pervasive in many various areas of biblical truth today. Remember, when we discuss hell, we aren't threatening to take away a theological plank in the doctrine of salvation. We are simply discussing the nature of hell, but some still get as mad as . . . well, you can imagine, about the subject.

"Jesus said more about hell than any other subject!" one Facebook comment said in all caps. The fact is that's just not true. Jesus talked more about the kingdom of God than He ever talked about hell. On a related matter, the Apostle Paul never even mentioned hell. That fact speaks volumes about its place in orthodox Christian thought. For that matter, the Old Testament never even hints of such a thing. If you believe that the whole Bible is inspired and that this is such a foundational topic, it seems strange that the entirety of the Old Covenant that has so much to say about Law and punishment for violating it never once mentions hell.

Then there's the other side of the issue, which suggests that the very idea of hell in any sense of the word should be rejected.

"The word 'hell' isn't even in the Bible!" Nigel said to me one day.

"Of course, it isn't, Nigel," I answered. "'Hell' is an English word; the Bible was written in Hebrew and Greek."

Of course, he meant there is no teaching about hell in the Scriptures. I understand the objection of people like Nigel.

They contend that the translations of the Greek words rendered "hell" in English Bibles shouldn't be there. It is true that there is no time when the word "hell" is an accurate translation. The translators in various versions would have better translated the Greek word *hades* or the Hebrew word *sheol* as "grave." Usually translated as "hell," Gehenna refers to a garbage dump outside Jerusalem. However, it is crucial to recognize that those temporal locations might be seen as metaphors for a greater reality.

Think about it this way: our consciousness, the awareness we possess now, doesn't die. We don't simply lapse into a state of nonbeing the instant we breathe our last breath. Like those who believe in Christ, those who want nothing to do with Him still have consciousness and must live somewhere. What happens to those who leave this world shaking their fist at God? They still exist, so what is the "place" in which they exist? Unless you take the viewpoint of Universalists, who believe that everybody immediately opens their eyes to the eternal bliss of heaven and changes their minds instantly, the word "hell" is as good a word as any to describe the place they find themselves.

Hell is both a place and a condition. It is a place in the sense that we all continue to live after our bodies have died. So, in that sense of the word, "hell" is real. "Do you believe in hell?" is a question that has to be qualified. I agree with those who believe there is no hell when they are talking about a punitive infernalism that God inflicts on some people, but I don't think those who leave this world with contempt towards God find their attitude instantly turning into worship the instant they die. The same person who stood on this side of the boundary between time and eternity is the person who stands on the other side. To go into eternity opposing God's love is nothing less than hell. Hold on to that thought, though, because I plan to tell you that hell might not be as far from heaven as you may think.[4]

HELL FIRE

The most frequently used word in relation to hell is the word "fire." The word is repeatedly used in the New Testament in connection with judgment. However, the question that needs consideration is, "What exactly is this fire?" Is it an expression of eternal anger from God, who has finally reached the end of His grace? Is it contemptuous rage toward those who refused to love Him after He had loved them?

Considering that this same God admonishes us to "Love your enemies, bless them that curse you, do good to them that hate you" (Matthew 5:44, KJV), how much sense does it make that He would do just the opposite? Does He call on us to behave more nobly toward those who oppose us than He does? Would He call us to live by a higher standard than He lives by? On the one hand, He is God and can do whatever He wants. On the other, does it make sense that He would ask us to do more than He is willing to do? And, even if He would ask that, by what power could we possibly do it? How would He expect us to do it if He won't do it? The whole argument breaks down when examined.

> "God is love," says 1 John 4:8. The
> God who told us to forgive
> seventy times seven (endlessly)
> behaves that way Himself. He
> never asks more of you than He is
> willing to do.

The Apostle Paul wrote that love "is not provoked, does not take into account a wrong suffered" (1 Corinthians 13:5). Is that true of the God who is love? Or does He not fit within this biblical description of love that He expects to be applied to everybody else? The Scripture assures us that "God was in Christ, reconciling the world to himself, no longer counting people's sins against them" (2 Corinthians 5:19). Since He doesn't count people's sins against them, what would be the cause for this divine rage that some imagine?

How, then, do we reconcile this fire with a God who is, by nature, love? Within a proper context, it can be done. Consider this verse in Hebrews 12:29: "Our God *is* a consuming fire" (emphasis added). God is fire. God is love. Therefore, that fire is love. The logic is clear. Would it change your view of hell if the fire were the experience of those in eternity who still loathe God as they are engulfed in divine love?

Consider this passage, in Isaiah 33:10-16:

[10] Now I will arise," says the LORD, "Now I will be exalted, now I will be lifted up. [11] You have conceived chaff; you will give birth to stubble; My breath will consume you like a fire. [12] The peoples will be burned to lime like cut thorns which are burned in the fire. [13] You who are far away, hear what I have done; And you who are near, acknowledge My might." [14] Sinners in Zion are terrified; Trembling has seized the godless. Who among us can live with the consuming fire? Who among us can live with continual burning? [15] He who walks righteously and speaks with sincerity, He who rejects unjust gain and shakes his hands so that they hold no bribe; He who stops his ears from hearing about bloodshed and shuts his eyes from looking upon evil; [16] He will dwell on the heights, His refuge will be the impregnable rock; His bread will be given him, His water will be sure.

What does Isaiah say about this fire? He says that some will experience it like cut thorns being burned. The description is indeed fearful. Sinners in Zion are terrified, and trembling has seized the godless. The best possible word to describe their plight is "hell."

However, others experience that same fire and relate to it quite differently. Isaiah focuses on them with the question, "Who among us can live with the consuming fire? Who among us can live with continual burning? Then he answers, "He who walks righteously and speaks with sincerity, He who rejects unjust gain and shuts his eyes from looking upon evil."

THE SUN NEVER CHANGES

Consider the sun and its rays as an analogy. To a flower in bloom, the sun's rays bring nourishment and life; they are essential for its growth and beauty. The same rays, however, can cause a withering effect on a piece of dry, brittle grass. The sun doesn't change its nature—it shines the same on the flower and the grass. The difference lies in the nature of what is receiving the sun's rays.

Similarly, the fire of God, as Isaiah 33:10-16 describes it, acts differently to different people. For those who are receptive, this divine fire is like the nourishing rays to a flower— purifying, refining, and bringing life. On the other hand, for those who reject His love, the same divine fire is experienced as a consuming and terrifying force, like the sun's rays scorching dry grass. Do you see the point here that the fire of God doesn't change—His love is constant. The experience of that fire, whether as nurturing warmth or consuming heat, depends on the state of our hearts in relation to God's unchanging nature of love.

Daniel 7:10 answers: "A river of fire was flowing, coming out from before him. Thousands upon thousands attended him; ten thousand times ten thousand stood before him" (NIV). Daniel saw The Ancient of Days (God) sitting on his throne, which was ablaze with flames. (SEE DANIEL 7:9) From that flaming throne flowed a river. In Daniel's vision, all the people are there in the presence of this river and the One from whom it flows.

There are no subdivisions in the eternal realm. In Daniels's vision, everybody was there, in the same place. Once we leave the temporal, we can only be in the eternal. And in that eternal realm, we all will meet God face-to-face. When we do, we will see that from His fiery throne gushes a river of flames.

> What is this river of fire? It is the raging outpouring of divine agape, and everybody is present. Depending on how they relate to God's love, it will be heaven to some and hell to others. Some receive His love, others reject it, but He loves nonetheless. What else is He to do as the God who is love?

Thomas Merton explained, "Our God is a consuming fire. And if we, by love, become transformed into Him and burn as He burns, his fire will be our everlasting joy. But if we refuse his love and remain in the coldness of sin and opposition to Him and to other men, then will His fire (by our choice rather than His) become our everlasting enemy, and Love, instead of being our joy, will become our torment and our destruction."[5]

Seventh-century theologian and Bishop Saint Isaac the Assyrian wrote, "I say, that those who are suffering in hell, are suffering in being scourged by love. It is totally false to think that the sinners in hell are deprived of God's love. Love is a child of the knowledge of truth and is unquestionably given commonly to all. But love's power acts in two ways: it torments sinners, while at the same time, it delights those who have lived in accord with it."[6]

The difference is in how the individual relates to divine love. It is not a matter of God having an attitude of loving acceptance toward those who believe and scornful rejection toward those who haven't. Our God's nature doesn't change one day because the grace clock finally runs down. "I am the LORD, and I do not change," He once told rebellious Israel. (See Malachi 3:6, NLT) If God is a God of loving grace now, and He is, then we have His guarantee that He won't change at some point in the future.

Reimagining hell as the fire of divine love challenges traditional notions of divine wrath and eternal punishment, reframing them in the context of God's unchanging love. This perspective doesn't diminish the reality of sin or its consequences but places them inside the greater narrative of God's redeeming passion for humanity. It suggests that God's ultimate desire is not condemnation but reconciliation, not endless punishment but the zealous desire that flows from His intense, all-consuming love. This view invites us to a deeper contemplation of the nature of divine love and its profound implications for both this life and the next world. In this light, the fire of hell is not a symbol of God's anger but a testament to His love's relentless and transformative power. Wrath isn't retaliatory but redemptive.

QUESTIONS FOR REFLECTION

1. Discuss the concept of divine wrath not as retributive anger but as passionate love. How does this reinterpretation affect your understanding of God's character?

2. The author suggests that our experience of God's wrath depends on our response to His love. Share thoughts or experiences that support or challenge this idea.

3. Reflect on the notion that hell could be an experience of being unable to accept God's love. How does this perspective shift your thoughts on eternal punishment?

4. In light of the chapter, how do you reconcile the biblical depictions of God's wrath with the message of God's unfailing love?

5. Consider the metaphor of the sun used in the chapter. Discuss how this metaphor helps understand the dual nature of God's wrath as both justice and love.

CHAPTER 4

FROM SINNERS TO SAINTS

A NEW PERSPECTIVE ON IDENTITY

I believe that there is no one so bad that he would be unable to become good all of a sudden, in an instant. — The Brothers Karamazov

In 1954, a single mother living in deep poverty in rural Mississippi gave birth to a baby girl. Because this young mother couldn't care for her, the child's grandmother brought the baby into her home. Living with her grandmother brought tremendous challenges. The child often wore dresses made from potato sacks, which led to bullying and ridicule from other children. At an early age, she began to be sexually abused by male relatives and acquaintances, including a cousin, an uncle, and a family friend. The abuse continued for several years and had a profound effect on her mental and emotional well-being.

Her early years were also characterized by instability because of her living arrangements. She was moved between family members, spending time with her grandmother, mother, and later her father. Each move brought its own set of disruptions and new problems.

At the age of 14, she became pregnant as a result of the sexual abuse she had suffered. The baby, a boy, was born prematurely and died shortly after birth. This event created a trauma in her that had a profound effect on her sense of self-worth.

Together, these adversities understandably gave her a very low opinion of herself. In her adult life, she has often said, "I felt like I wasn't wanted as a child from the time I was a child." Thankfully, as she entered her teen years, things began to change when she cultivated a love for reading. This habit would become the foundation of her future trajectory. Through the books she read, her mind began to change. She began to realize that she was more than the things she experienced. She began to see herself not as a poor child with no hope but as one who could lay hold of great possibility. Her self-image gradually transformed for the better. As an adult, she has spoken about the journey of self-discovery, the importance of understanding one's value, and how that kind of self-discovery can transform a life.

The young girl I speak of is the woman you know as Oprah Winfrey. In various interviews discussing her life, Oprah has said, "I don't think of myself as a poor, deprived ghetto girl who made good. I think of myself as somebody who, from an early age, knew I was responsible for myself."

She has spoken extensively about the power of self-belief and how changing her perception was pivotal in her success. In her own words, she has often said, "Create the highest, grandest vision possible for your life because you become what you believe."

"You become what you believe." A Bible verse suggests the same thing – a text often associated with the idea that our thoughts or self-perceptions shape our lives. It's found in Proverbs 23:7. In the *King James Version*, it reads: "For as he thinketh in his heart, so is he..." This part of the verse suggests a clear connection between a person's thoughts or inner beliefs and actions.

Sadly, the modern world of Christendom often teaches a message that debilitates people in many ways. What is this message that does such harm? It's the teaching that we are "just sinners saved by grace."

On the surface, because of the biased context in which we've heard that statement, it can sound humble to make that statement. It can seem to give God credit for accepting us when, by every standard we've been taught, we were unacceptable. The problem is that this viewpoint leaves people with the sense that something is fundamentally wrong with them. Ask the average church member, and they'll tell you that they are still a sinner, but because of God's grace, He loves them anyway.

There are some problems with that view. First, it's not biblical – at least not in the way most people understand sin. Second, it leaves people seeing themselves as less than they are, and nobody will consistently live at a higher level than their sense of identity permits.

Almost thirty years ago, I wrote the following illustration in my book, *Grace Walk*: "When I was a student in high school, a hypnotist came to our science class. He brought four students to the front of the room and hypnotized them together. While they were in a trance, he told them that they would each be an animal when they woke up. One boy was told that he would be a monkey. Another would wake up as a dog. One girl would be a chicken, and the other a turkey. The hypnotist said, 'I will count to five and snap my fingers, and you will wake up when I do.' He slowly counted to five, snapped his fingers, and they woke up like he had said.

What happened next was quite a sight. They behaved exactly like the animals they had been told they would become. One hopped around and all stooped, his hands swinging like a monkey. He jumped up on a desk and screeched like a Cheetah. The other boy started barking and running around the room like a dog. The first girl folded her hands under her arms and clucked as if she were trying to lay eggs. The other strutted around like a turkey, gobbling as loud as she could and scratching at the floor with both hands. Seeing people act like the animals they thought they were was a comical sight. After a while, the hypnotist wakes them up and lets them come back to their real identities. You can imagine how embarrassed they were when we told them how they had behaved."[1]

What you think about yourself will be the greatest determinant of how you live your life. If you think you are just "a sinner saved by grace," then you will forever be trying to overcome what you believe to be your natural inclinations. You will be your own worst enemy. Some who have been brainwashed think it somehow honors God to see themselves in this negative way. They believe it makes God look better for them to look worse, but that is not the case at all. It contradicts how God sees you, and let's be clear: the way God sees something or somebody is the way it is. To dispute what He says about us is an insult. Imagine speaking with contempt about the painting of a renowned artist to his face. That's precisely what we do with God every time we speak of ourselves in the self-deprecating way that has become so common in the church world.

What Does It Mean To Be A Sinner?

In the New Testament, the Greek word for sin, *hamartia*, is often interpreted as "missing the mark." However, this raises the question: what exactly is the mark being missed?

Traditionally, many in the Western church perceive God through the legal paradigm we discussed earlier when examining His justice and wrath. Because they misunderstand His nature, they define sin as falling short of a moral standard they wrongly imagine God to have set. However, this perspective is limiting to us, especially considering that Jesus referred to God not as a Judge but as a Father—Abba. If we think of God as a judge, then we're likely to see sin as a crime, which it is not.

Francois Du Toit, known for his stellar work on the *Mirror Study Bible*, offers the orthodox interpretation of *hamartia*. He breaks down the word into two parts: *ha*, meaning negate, and *martia*, derived from *meros*, which means form or identity. Together, the prefix and root of the word means "no form."[2]

A correct understanding of "sin" refers to denying or negating our true identity. It's about missing the essence of our true nature, to come short of seeing ourselves the way God sees us. "All have sinned and come short of the glory of God" (Romans 3:23). To sin is to come short of God's glory. What is this glory of which the Bible speaks? The word's original root is *doxa*, which means "opinion," you can be sure God's opinion of you isn't negative. Every use of the word in the New Testament is positive.[3] To sin, then, is to fail to see ourselves as God sees us. Remember, however, God sees you is the way you are.

> Do you understand how seeing your-
> self as "just a sinner saved by
> grace" is an insult to God's
> opinion of you? Once we know
> the true meaning of the word
> "sin," we recognize that "sinner"
> isn't a word describing crime but
> confusion about who we are.

In that sense of the word, every one of us has sinned, and many still do. We sin by seeing ourselves still being sinners saved by grace. Just as Adam lost sight of his authentic self after the fall in the garden, many today don't know who they are. They live "in sin" (*hamartia*) in the truest sense of the word by having "no identity" that aligns with God's opinion (*doxa*) of them. Many of those are professing believers in Christ who still don't know their true identity. They think they're just sinners saved by grace. It's a sad and debilitating predicament. It "hobbles" them in their grace walk.[4] That's what legalistic religion does by teaching people that they are nothing more than sinners saved by grace.

There is a sense of the word in which it would be accurate to say that people are still sinners if, by definition, we mean that many don't understand the truth of who they are. They "come short" when understanding themselves as defined by God's assessment of them. For all have sinned and come short of the glory (assessment) of God." However, the use of the word in the modern church world seldom follows that definition. The common understanding of the meaning of sin in the Evangelical world is grounded in morality, which is not at all in alignment with the word's original meaning. "Sins" are simply the bitter fruit of sin. People do wrong because they believe wrong things about themselves and act accordingly.

In the orthodox sense of the word, as it is used in the Bible, you are not a sinner. Emancipation from seeing ourselves in such a contaminated way sets us free to live the life we were created to know and enjoy. How do we know our authentic identity? Think of it like this:

YOU ARE A TREASURE

Suppose I found a diamond ring in the parking lot where I go to buy groceries. I could go back inside the store and ask the manager if anybody had reported losing their ring. When she tells me nobody has reported it, I leave my phone number and go home with the ring.

After a month, I came to realize that nobody was going to claim that ring. It's mine, and now I begin to ask the obvious question anybody would ask: "What is this thing worth?" Maybe I take it with me when I meet a friend for lunch and show it to him. "That's not real," he says. "It's cubic zirconium. Probably worth a couple of hundred dollars but not a real diamond."

Later, I show it to somebody else, who says, "Ha! That's one of those rings you can buy at novelty stores! It's plastic! You have found yourself a five-dollar imitation!" I leave him, and another person says, "Oh, wow! You have found a nice diamond! My sister has one just like it, and I know she paid almost ten thousand dollars for hers!"

What am I to believe? The opinions I've been given range from trash to treasure. How am I to know? The answer is simple. I'll take the ring to a jeweler and ask him to give me an appraisal. He will determine its value based on what the ring would sell for in the open market. If he tells me that the ring is worth ten thousand dollars, it's because he knows somebody will pay that price for it. Plainly put, the ring equals ten thousand dollars.

In life, people often tend to determine their personal value in a similar way as I've described with the ring. What do other people think about me? If I ask my employer, I will get one answer, but if I ask my mother, the answer will be totally different. Different people value me at different levels. How am I to know? By doing the same thing one would do with the ring: Ask the expert.

The Bible says that you have been bought with a price. (SEE 1 CORINTHIANS 6:20 AND 7:23) The way to know your actual value is to ask the One who bought you. Your Creator thought you were worth giving His very life for so that you would know who you are and whose you are. He thought it worth dying, not to change your worth, but to prove it to you. Your worth, then, equals the life of Jesus Christ Himself.

One parable Jesus told describes a man who knew about a treasure in a field, and he wanted that treasure so much that he sold everything he had to be able to buy the field just to have the treasure. That person is Christ. The field is the world, and you are the treasure. He gave everything for you. Stop calling yourself a sinner saved by grace as if you're somehow a piece of junk that God was kind enough to pick up off a trash pile out of the goodness of His heart. You are a treasure.

Who are you? Ask the only One who truly knows. He is the one who made you and holds you as His own. What does He say about who you are?

YOU ARE A WORK OF ART

The Bible says, "For we are His workmanship, created in Christ Jesus for good works, which God prepared beforehand so that we would walk in them" (Ephesians 2:10). The Greek word translated "workmanship" is *poema*, the word from which we get our English word "poem." It means a masterfully crafted object, like a piece of poetry, a painting, or a sculpture. In other words, you are God's work of art!

Don't confuse humility with a religious inferiority complex somebody has laid on you. You are a valuable work of art to the One who created you. It doesn't honor Him for you to disagree with what He says about you. It isn't prideful to accept His assessment of your value. Stop sinning by denying your true form – a person created in the image of God and indwelt the very Spirit of Christ.[5]

You Are A Saint

In 1 Corinthians 1:2, Paul addresses the people of the church at Corinth as saints. He certainly had to be talking about an identity that stemmed from their spiritual birth because their behavior wasn't saintly. Their behavior included prejudice and discrimination, misogyny, gluttony, sexual immorality, drunkenness, religious arrogance, and many other things that weren't very "Christian," but Paul recognized that their behavior didn't define them. God did.

In Chapter 1, he calls them saints and then spends the rest of his letter telling them to live like the saints they are. Don't be uncomfortable being called a saint because that's what God calls you! That doesn't mean you live a flawlessly perfect life, but it does mean that God has set you apart and placed the nature of Christ within you. Understanding that reality is a miraculously liberating truth that can "all of a sudden, in an instant" transform from seeing yourself as a fundamentally bad person to one who is good, not because of anything you have done or not done but because of Christ.

You Are Accepted

You don't have to score religious brownie points with God. You're in. You are accepted because you are in Christ (See Ephesians 1:6). Since the Father fully accepts Him, you are entirely accepted too! You don't need to change a thing about yourself for God to accept you. Your acceptance isn't based on what you do but on who you are. Ironically, when a person realizes that fact, changes start to come into his life.

Religion says we must change for God to embrace us, but grace is the good news that God has already embraced us, just as we are now. If you never change, He still loves and accepts you, but I'll let you in on a secret that religion misses: Knowing how much you're loved and accepted becomes the catalyst for a desire to change. It won't be rules but awareness of your relationship with Him that moves you toward transformation. More will be said about that in the next chapter, but for now, know that you are 100% accepted by God no matter what you're doing or not doing.

These few items are just the starting point. You may think, "But I don't think of myself as a heavenly poem. I don't feel like a saint. I know how I act sometimes and don't feel accepted by God." I get it. Any honest person would but the heart of the matter revolves around who you will trust.

Back to the diamond illustration – will you believe what somebody else says about your value? Who can you trust to be accurate? Everybody will have their own bias. Until you know better, even you will base your sense of identity on your past experiences and the voice that has spoken into your life.

> There comes a time in every person's journey when, if we are to continue to grow, we must rise above our upbringing – what we learned from our nuclear family, what we've been told in church, what friends and foes have said about us, what we were taught in school, what our behavior would suggest and what culture at large tells us. We must come back to Source, the One from whom we originate. We must look to our Eternal Father to inform us of who we are and believe what He says.

Do you see that you aren't just a sinner saved by grace? Our actual value and identity don't come from our behavior, achievements, or the various opinions of others. Instead, it is a constant, deeply rooted in the divine assessment made by our Creator. What He says goes. Just as a diamond's worth isn't determined by the opinions of ordinary people, but by the expert's appraisal, so is our worth defined by God's perfect evaluation of us.

God's declaration over your life is clear and unequivocal: you have been bought at a price that reflects the highest form of love and sacrifice — the life of Jesus Christ Himself. He didn't do it to make you worthy but because He saw you as worthy.

"But I don't deserve it!" you may protest. Legalistic religion nurtures that mindset in people. The church world is filled with people confessing, "I'm not worthy! I'm not worthy!" On the surface, it sounds so humble, but it's not. Although it is a sincere confession, it doesn't come from or resonate with the heart of God. It's a religious inferiority complex that prompts that kind of statement.

"Are you saying we *are* worthy?" one might ask in disbelief. No, that is not what I'm saying. What's important to under-stand here is that the whole worthy/unworthy approach is a categorical error.

Think of it like this: What if your child kept saying such a thing to you? Imagine your child saying, "I'm not worthy! I don't deserve your love. You are so good to me to feed me, clothe me, and give me a place to live. I don't deserve it! Thank you for accepting me! Thank you for loving me!"

If your child said that to you, you would shake your head and think, "Whoa. We need to get this kid some therapy. Something has jumped track here!" You see how ridiculous it looks in this situation. This is your child! Neither worthiness nor unworthiness have anything to do with it. You love your child because that is your child. It has nothing to do with deserving or not deserving. The same is true with God. He is your Heavenly Father. Who can know His response when we put ourselves down and speak to Him in terms of not being deserving? I know it would concern me as a parent if my children did that, so I can only imagine that He might shake His head when we do it. I imagine He must think to Himself, "I so want them to understand they are Mine, and I love to accept them for no other reason!"

It's not about worth. It's about love,
     which Jesus died to show us.
     Some think they're unworthy, "but
     God demonstrates His own love
     toward us, in that while we were
     still sinners (totally unaware of
     our true form, created in His
     image), Christ died for us"
     (Romans 5:8). This profound act
     isn't a transaction to change us; it
     is a testament to challenge us to
     see our worth in the eyes of the
     One who created us.

You are a treasure, not because of what you have done or what you may achieve, but because you are a divine creation crafted by the hands of God. You are His workmanship, His masterpiece (Ephesians 2:10), a unique expression of His creativity and love. In understanding this, we must shift our perspective from seeing ourselves through the lens of our flaws and failures to viewing ourselves as God sees us — valuable, cherished, and imbued with His Spirit. You are not a sinner. You know better now. You are a saint.

As you move deeper into that understanding, embrace your authentic identity with confidence and gratitude. Walk in the assurance that your value is unchangeable in the eyes of your Heavenly Father. In this realization, you will find the freedom to live fully, love deeply, and grow into the expression of who you were created to be.

Remember, your worth isn't up for debate; it is a divine declaration, a sacred truth that stands eternal, and nobody – not even you – is strong enough to change that.

QUESTIONS FOR REFLECTION

1. How does the redefinition of sin as "missing the mark" of our true identity challenge traditional views of sinfulness?
2. The author argues that seeing ourselves as "just sinners saved by grace" can be limiting. Discuss the

implications of this viewpoint on personal growth and spiritual development.

3. Share a personal experience where recognizing your identity in Christ led to a significant change in your life or perspective.

4. How does understanding our identity as God sees us empower us to live more fully in His love and grace?

5. Reflect on the statement, "You become what you believe." Discuss how this principle has played out in your understanding of your spiritual identity.

CHAPTER 5

FROM MORAL LIVING TO MIRACULOUS LIVING

A NEW PERSPECTIVE ON LIFE

To love another person is to see the face of God - Les Misérables

Imagine that one morning, after he had eaten the forbidden fruit, Adam was awakened by Eve leaning over him and kissing him gently on the cheek. "Good morning, my sweetheart," she whispered. "I brought you breakfast in bed this morning. You seemed to be resting so well that I let you sleep late today."

Adam opened his eyes, looked at Eve, and snarled at her in anger: "What do you mean waking me up, woman? Couldn't you see that I was asleep? How dare you! What have you shoved under my nose? A bowl of fruit? You've already caused me enough trouble with fruit! Get out of my face!"

Shocked, Eve's eyes filled with tears, and she ran off to a secluded place where she could cry alone. By mid-morning, Adam felt guilty about how he had treated his wife. He found her and humbly approached her. "Eve, I am so sorry. It was so wrong for me to behave that way. It was simply evil! Please forgive me. I wouldn't blame you if you left me for another…well, anyway, you get the point." Eve looked up through teary eyes as Adam continued. "Eve, I promise I will make it up to you. Tomorrow will be your special day. Listen, world! Tomorrow is Eve Day on Planet Earth," he shouted.

True to his word, Adam treated Eve like a queen the next day. He pampered her all day long. That night, when she went to bed, he gently leaned across her, kissed her on the cheek, and said, "Good night, my dear princess. I'm so blessed to have you as my wife." "Oh, Adam, you're so good to me," she cooed.

Now, it's time to take a short test to determine the basis you use to determine what guides your lifestyle. There are only two questions on this test. Your answer to these questions will reveal whether you tend to see life primarily through the lens of religion or through the lens of your relationship with God.

1. Was God pleased with Adam's actions on the first day of the story?

2. Was God pleased with Adam's actions on the
    second day of the story?

The answer to both questions is no. God was not pleased on either day.[1] Adam's behavior was evil on the first day and good on the second day. So how is it possible that God still wasn't satisfied when he stopped behaving in the wrong way and started behaving the right way? It has to do with one truth that most churches not only don't teach but instead teach the opposite about when it comes to our lifestyles.

> The truth is that God doesn't set morality as the standard for our lifestyles. It's not about good and bad behavior. Don't freak out about that statement. I'm not suggesting that it's okay to live an immoral lifestyle. The fact is that the metrics of morality and immorality aren't measurements that God uses with us. You are capable of much more than morality. You have the ability to live miraculously.

Regardless of which church you attend next week, you will likely hear the same kind of teaching. While the details would be different, the flow would go something like this:

1. There's something you aren't doing that you should be doing. (That might mean that you should stop doing something wrong.)
2. God isn't happy about that, so you need to change it.
3. Dedicate yourself to God and promise Him that you'll try harder (with His help) to do better.

The hook of the sermon is the promise that if you do this, then you will become more like Christ, and, after all, who doesn't want to be more like Him? If you are a discerning reader, you recognize that was a loaded question. "Who doesn't want to be more like Christ?" It sounds like a noble question on the surface, but the fact is that you are already like Him. The Apostle Peter wrote that you share His very nature. (SEE 2 PETER 1:4)

Let's go back to the story of Adam and Eve to lay the foundation for this truth. At the very beginning, the Trinity said, "Let us make man in our own image" (Genesis 1:26). "Then the Lord God formed a man from the dust of the ground and breathed into his nostrils the breath of life, and the man became a living being" (Genesis 2:7). What was the "breath of life" that God breathed into him? It was the life of God Himself. God breathed Himself into Adam.

The name "Adam" means "from the earth" or "of the ground" and is usually understood to refer to humanity in the broader sense.[2] God created humanity and breathed Himself into the human race in such a way that he defined us. After creating everything, including man, God observed all that He had made and found it to be "very good." (SEE GENESIS 1:31)

> God's purpose in creating people was
> that He might enjoy them,
> expressing His loving nature to
> them and through them.

He lovingly placed Adam and Eve in the Garden of Eden and gave them reign over the Garden and everything in it.

Inside the garden were two trees situated in the very middle. "And out of the ground the LORD God made every tree grow that is pleasant to the sight and good for food. The tree of life was also in the midst of the garden and the tree of the knowledge of good and evil" (Genesis 2:9). Two trees formed the matrix for the whole concept of morality.

THE TREE OF LIFE

The Tree of Life speaks for itself. Remember that God breathed into Adam the breath of life. He then placed the tree of life in the middle of this garden. It's right in the middle – a focal point of the garden, so it must be important. What is the meaning of this tree?

A basic principle of biblical interpretation is that the Old Testament scriptures are to be understood in light of New Testament revelation. The key word that defines this tree is "life." A quick search of the New Testament makes it clear that Jesus Christ is the source and center of life. This same God who breathed life into Adam in the Old Testament incarnates as one of us in the New Testament.

The Tree of Life foreshadows Jesus Christ, Divine Love personified. God intended that Adam and Eve should live by His life all their days. As long as He was their only source in this world, questions of right and wrong would never have arisen. A moral framework would have been irrelevant because Divine Life and Love would have governed his every thought and deed. Eating from the second tree is where the trouble for mankind began.

Their instructions were clear: "You are free to eat from any tree in the garden, but you must not eat from the tree of the knowledge of good and evil, for when you eat from it, you will certainly die" (Genesis 2:16-17). Note that God didn't say He would kill them as punishment for eating from the tree. Eating from the tree is what would cause them to die, not God. Don't think that it is God who punishes us for our misbehavior. Sins (acting in a way that demonstrates we have lost sight of our true identity) bring their own punishment.

THE TREE OF THE KNOWLEDGE OF GOOD AND EVIL

Of all the trees with fruit in the garden, there was only one that Adam and Eve were forbidden to eat. It was the Tree of the Knowledge of Good and Evil. The prohibition was for their good. Eating from the Tree of Life would nurture the Life God had breathed into them. However, they were told they would die on the day they ate from the Tree of the Knowledge of Good and Evil. So, the choice was clear—life or death. They could continue to live in total dependence on God or choose independence from Him.

The third chapter of Genesis records the story of how humanity fell. Imagine the scene. Here they were, in the lush paradise of Eden, where everything existed in perfect harmony. Then comes the day Eve walks through the garden when the forbidden tree catches her attention. She walks over to the tree and begins to examine it more closely. What a lovely tree. What beautiful fruit.

Soon, she becomes aware of a serpent who slithered up to her side and began to whisper to her in a hushed, honeyed tone: "God won't let you eat from these trees, will he?"

"Oh, we can eat from all of the trees except this one," Eve answered. "If we eat from this tree, we will die."

"You certainly will not die," the serpent seductively said to the woman. For God knows that when you eat from it your eyes will be opened, and you will be like God" (Genesis 3:4-5).

"Be like God?" Eve must have thought to herself. "What could possibly be wrong with that? I do want to be more Godlike!" she reasoned. Then she reached out, her hand trembling with excitement, the air thick with anticipation. The fruit felt smooth to her touch, its skin beautiful and inviting. Slowly, she brought the fruit to her lips. Everything in heaven and earth came to a standstill, waiting for the moment that would redefine human existence. She bit.

Then, a short time later, she shared that same fruit with Adam, and everything changed. Whereas they had lived from understanding their union with God, now that awareness had died. Before, they had been perfectly content with who they were, but now that clear knowledge of their authentic identity had died. Upon examining themselves, they concluded that they weren't acceptable, so they made coverings for their bodies.

Before, they had reveled in a life of love with their Creator and each other; now, their joy died, and shame sent them into hiding, believing the crippling lie that God becomes angry with people when they sin. The shift in how they perceived God changed how they saw each other. Adam had seen Eve as "bone of my bones and flesh of my flesh," but now he blamed her for his transgression. (SEE GENESIS 3:12) No longer did he see the face of God in her but saw in Eve a scapegoat for his own wrongdoing.

So much died that day. Their disobedience completely changed them. However, it is so very important to understand the other side of the equation in this story. Their sin did not change God. Everything changed with them, but nothing changed with God. His disposition toward them was exactly the same. When Adam hid, God came for their evening walk, just as He had always done. God always acts toward restoration.

Their disobedience mutilated Adam and Eve. They were murdered by it, but we must understand this: It was a mental mutilation and murder. They were the same people God had made them to be, but they lost sight of their original image. They wrongly believed that now they were alienated from God and had become His enemy. That same lie has infected humanity since that day. Religious people not only still believe it but perpetuate the lie. They don't believe that nothing can separate us from the love of God.

Paul wrote about this problem to one confused church, "And you, that were sometime alienated and enemies *in your mind* by wicked works, yet now hath he reconciled" (Colossians 1:21, KJV, emphasis added). It was all in their minds!

The word "repentance" is pivotal in matters like this. Its meaning is "to change your mind," and the implication is that repentance is a radical change of mind. It denotes the idea of moving in an opposite direction. That kind of repentance is needed in the church world today that unwittingly promotes the lie that God is angry about humanity's sin. If the incarnation of Jesus Christ proves anything, it shows us that God isn't angry but loves us so much that He came here as a human being to show us how much He loves and has always loved us. He came to save us from the lie.

MORALITY'S MESS

While the Tree of Life offered life, the Tree of the Knowledge of Good and Evil provided knowledge. What kind of knowledge did it offer? The knowledge of good and evil. It provided the ability to know right from wrong. They gained that knowledge when Adam and Eve ate the fruit from that tree. Until then, they hadn't possessed it. Why? Because they didn't need it. Their lifestyles were miraculous as long as they lived out of their union with their Creator. Divine Live flowed in and through them. They breathed the divine breath exhaled into them from the beginning. They lived His Life as their Creator animated their lifestyles. Their practice of living out of Oneness was all they needed. It's all we've ever needed. It's all we still need.

When the serpent enticed Eve into eating from the Tree of the Knowledge of Good and Evil, his seduction was that she would "become like God, knowing good from evil." Note the subtlety of that lie. "You will become like God." It sounds good, but wait a minute! Eve was already like God! She and Adam had been created in His image, and God had declared they were "very good!" (SEE GENESIS 1:31)

> Here's an important thing to note: The first sin ever committed by a human was when somebody tried to do the right thing. She was deceived and didn't intend to do wrong. She meant to do right because she believed a lie. She lost sight of her authentic identity as one who was created in the image of God and having forgotten that, she tried to do something to improve herself.

The first sin committed by a human being resulted from believing the first lie ever told in this world. The first lie ever spoken on planet Earth was when the serpent told Eve there was something she could do to become more like God. She was already like God.

Fast forward to the 21st Century and consider what is being taught in churches everywhere today. People are constantly being told that there are things they can do to be more like Christ. Although nobody is trying to mislead others, it is the same lie told in the Garden of Eden.

The fact is that you are already like Christ. You share His very nature. (2 Peter 1:4) You are one with Him. (1 Corinthians 6:17) Your very existence finds its source in Him. (Acts 17:28) You don't even have a life of your own, but His life defines you. (Galatians 2:20)

The delusion that we are flawed and need to try harder to do better denies the New Testament teaching about our true selves and spits in the face of Grace. We aren't to live by morals but by the miraculous indwelling life of Christ. God could have told Adam and Eve to eat from the good branch but stay away from the evil branch on the Tree of the Knowledge of Good and Evil, but that's not what He said. He told them to leave it alone altogether.

Remember the imaginary scenario at the beginning of this chapter? In the first scenario, Adam was hateful toward Eve. He did wrong. In the second scenario, he was kind toward her. Nobody could deny that he did right. The thing to recognize is that he changed his behavior from evil to good, but on both days, he was still up the wrong tree!

> God's intention isn't that we live a lifestyle of morality based on right and wrong. We don't need to change branches. We need to change trees.

Don't ever rededicate yourself to God and promise Him that you'll try harder to do better. That's not what He wants and is, in fact, right out of the serpent's playbook. Instead, abandon yourself to His loving care and ask Him to live His life through you. It's not a determined undertaking but a divine union that is the pathway to the lifestyle you are meant to know and enjoy.

Good and evil are a ditch on each side of that Morality Road. Don't travel there. Even good behavior that doesn't express Christ within us is a sin. Remember that sin (*hamartia*) is the condition of not knowing our true form. When we don't know who we are, we sin by trying to change branches. We promise God we'll stop doing wrong things and start doing right (often religious) things. That isn't what He wants. The serpent in the garden wanted that, but it has never been what God wanted.

Perhaps it's time to "go to church" together as the chapter comes to a close. It might help some if I meet you on your home turf. It's time for the call to repentance. You've heard many invitations for people to repent of immorality, but this one is to challenge repentance from morality. Good and evil are the impetus for morality and immorality, and you need neither. What we all need is to recognize the union we share with Christ. We need to realize that we are already like Him and can do nothing to become more Christlike. Our behavior can become more Christlike, and it will to the extent that we know who we are. We must realize that God is not, nor has He ever been, against us, angry toward us, or even disappointed in us.

How could He be disappointed? The One who created you has always known everything about you, even before you were born. Knowing all there is to know – the good, the bad, and the ugly – He wants you for Himself. Nothing you've ever done or could do will change His mind about you.

Abandon the pursuit of moral living and accept the prize of miraculous living. Don't focus on yourself, but focus on Him. You are better than you were probably told and don't need to become more Christlike. You already are like Christ, and it doesn't depend on your willpower to realize that in how you live your life. The one who has called you to this life will be faithful to finish what He has begun in you. It's not up to you to make it happen, and you'll wear yourself out trying. Stop trying harder and start trusting Him. It is a liberating day when a person is set free from the tyranny of trying and abandons herself to the Grace that grows us in nothing less than miraculous ways.

QUESTIONS FOR REFLECTION

1. How does the shift from a focus on morality to miraculous living redefine the Christian experience according to the author?

2. Discuss the potential pitfalls of viewing the Christian life primarily as "sin-management." How does this approach limit our understanding of grace?

3. Share a personal story where you experienced the miraculous in everyday life. How did this experience shift your focus from moral living to living in grace?

4. The author suggests that living miraculously involves trusting in God's ongoing work in us rather than our efforts. How does this perspective challenge or support your current spiritual practices?

5. Reflect on the idea that miracles are not just extraordinary events but also include the transformation of our hearts and minds. Discuss how this broader understanding of miracles can influence our daily lives.

CHAPTER 6

FROM GUILT TO GRACE

A NEW PERSPECTIVE ON FORGIVENESS

The quality of mercy is not strained; It droppeth as the gentle rain from heaven upon the place beneath. — The Merchant of Venice

In John Bunyan's *The Pilgrim's Progress*, the protagonist Christian carries a heavy burden, symbolizing sin, on his back. It is a terrible burden that causes him much pain and hardship. In one scene of Christian's journey, he arrives at the foot of the cross. As he stands there, looking at the cross, the straps of the burden suddenly break, and the weighty bundle falls from his back, rolls down a hill, and disappears into an empty tomb. Bunyan used this moment to symbolize the release of sin and guilt through the liberating power of Christ's sacrifice. Christian's relief and newfound freedom at this point were profound and marked a monumental turning point in his spiritual journey.

> After counseling people for many
>   decades, I can state unequivocally
>   that the most debilitating problem
>   that seems to hold people down is
>   a crippling sense of guilt.

Feelings of guilt accompanied by shame do more to drain zest for life than most can imagine. Although Bunyan wrote *The Pilgrim's Progress* in the late 1600s, modern scientific research validates that his story is more than allegorical.

In one study, researchers found evidence that the emotional experience of guilt can produce a sense of weight in the body. Their report said: "People often say guilt is like a 'weight on one's conscience,' and we examined whether guilt is actually embodied as a sensation of weight. In a series of studies, we asked students and members of the public to recall a time that they did something unethical. People recalled a variety of wrongdoings, such as lying, stealing, or cheating. Afterward, in a separate task, we asked them to rate their subjective feeling of their own body weight as compared to their average. That is, did they feel less weight than usual, about the same weight, or more weight? We compared these responses to participants in control conditions who recalled an ethical memory, a memory of someone else's unethical actions, or who were not asked to recall a memory.[1]

Did people actually report a sensation of more weight? We found that recalling personal unethical acts led participants to report increased subjective body weight as compared to recalling ethical acts, unethical acts of others, or no recall. We also found that this increased sense of weight was related to participants' heightened feelings of guilt and not other negative emotions, such as sadness or disgust. Although people sometimes associate importance with 'heaviness,' we found no evidence that importance could explain this finding."[2] It is interesting that the findings of this Princeton University report demonstrated how people often actually *feel* the weight of wrongdoing. Rarely have I met someone who has come for counseling who hasn't felt that weight in one way or another.

Having worked In a Christian environment all my life, it would seem likely that those who have heard and understand forgiveness wouldn't bear this burden. After all, haven't they, like Bunyan's "Christian" seen the cross and known the experience of having the straps break loose so that the burden of sin rolls down the hill into the empty tomb? Sadly, that is often not the case.

The legalistic world of the modern church often actually commoditizes guilt and shame rather than cure it. Nothing builds repeat business like leaving people with

feelings of deficit while leading
them to believe that you alone
have the answer to their problem.

That's why so many professing Christians are stuck in an
endless loop of self-degradation, spiritual rededication, and
shallow motivation to try harder to do better. It's an
unending cycle from which there is no hope of escape apart
from finally coming to understand authentic grace. They are
abused by religion that tells them they need to do something
about their sins.

From the moment Adam felt guilt and shame and crafted a
covering from leaves, those who are dead to the true
meaning of grace still try to do something to make themselves more presentable to God. The first lie told in the
garden, that there is something that can be done to become
godlier, is the theme of most modern sermons in legalistic
churches.

Growing up in a conservative corner of Christendom, I am
personally familiar with how it works. I was a pastor for the
first twenty-one years of my adult life. The template I used
for my sermons is common in legalistic churches of every
denomination.[3] The template always first points to guilt
among the congregants and then calls for action that
involves a commitment to do better.

The problem is that, no matter how hard people try, it's never enough because rules-keeping-religion never runs out of rules. To make matters worse, it constantly moves the goal post. "Okay, so you did better this week but *did you do enough?*" It's the damnable doctrine of dedication that suggests that the problem is on the believer's end when, in reality, the problem is that the message being promoted is a lie. "You shall know the truth, and the truth shall set you free," said Jesus. Lies, on the other hand, do just the opposite. They bind people. Have the sermons you've heard set you free from a sense of need to keep rededicating yourself to do better? Or do you think there's still something you need to do to get right with God? Any lie that suggests you're carrying guilt and need to deal with it is a rejection of the finished work of Christ. To believe it is to embrace religious idolatry.

The etymology of the word "religion" is commonly traced back to the Latin word *religio*. There are various interpretations of its root meaning, but a prominent one suggests that it comes from *religare*, which translates to "to bind." In the positive sense of the word, we are told it is used to bind people to something greater, particularly God. But is that even true? Does religion bind people to God? Of course not. Christ has done that. It does, however, bind unwitting victims to rules they can never keep. The result is a perpetual sense of deficiency fueled by a sense of guilt. The only answer most people are given is to rededicate themselves and try again, but that remedy never works. If it did people wouldn't need to keep doing it over and over again, many for all their lives. You know what they say about the definition of insanity.

Most people who grew up in the world of religion have been so indoctrinated with a sense of guilt that it feels like arrogance to suggest otherwise. They wrongly associate guilt and shame with their understanding of humility and believe it somehow honors God to put themselves down. They will say that they believe Jesus Christ took away their sins and then turn right around and argue that they are still sinners who constantly need forgiveness.

This contradictory viewpoint leads them to constantly judge themselves to be guilty and provokes them to try to do something about it. The "something" they do is always a religious act. Maybe it's a prayer of rededication, promising to try harder to do better. Maybe it's taking the sacraments or going to confession (the liturgical version of "rededicating your life to Christ" in the Evangelical world.") It doesn't matter what they do, the point is that they try to do something to "get right with God," and therein resides the idolatry. Why do I choose the word, "idolatry?" It's because to do something in an effort to "get right" presumes that we *aren't* right. It implies that the finished work of Jesus Christ isn't enough and that our religious works are necessary. It puts pious effort alongside, if not in front of, what Christ Jesus accomplished in His death. Those feelings of guilt and shame are a subtle, sinister way we try to help atone for our sins. He died but at least *we feel guilty too*!

While this sort of idolatry is prevalent in legalistic religion, it reaches much further out. Self-punishment is a common strategy that people employ to try to bypass the cross of Christ. The American Psychological Association reported on one study that demonstrates how people choose to inflict pain on themselves as the result of guilt. In this experiment, undergraduate students were asked to recall experiences that induced feelings of guilt, sadness, or neutral emotions (like grocery shopping). In the experiment's second part, these participants were given the option to self-administer electric shocks of varying intensities. Interestingly, those who had recalled feeling guilty were more likely to choose higher, mildly painful shock levels. This behavior indicates a tendency to self-punish in response to guilt.[4]

The National Library of Medicine reported on another that shows self-punishment demonstrated through self-denied pleasure. The authors call this tendency for self-punishment the Dobby Effect, a phenomenon named after the head-banging elf in the Harry Potter books that refers to a psychological tendency for people to employ self-punishment to ward off feelings of guilt. This scientific research shows a "widely held conviction that atonement absolves sins" (their words, not mine).[5]

With all due respect and recognition that sometimes people don't know better, it must be noted that anytime somebody still thinks they're carrying sin and need to do something to get rid of it, they are wandering toward idolatry. They are putting their own perceived ability to "get right with God" on something they think they can do instead of what Christ has already done. Like Christian in *The Pilgrim's Progress*, they are carrying a heavy load, and it's a load that affects people in more ways than most know. "The burden of sin" is more than a metaphor. Although the burden has indeed been removed, guilt brings a debilitating weight with it.

The problem of guilt becomes exponentially worse when it morphs into shame. Guilt is the recognition of having done wrong but shame is even worse because it insists that, not only have you done wrong, you *are* wrong. Guilt points to conduct but shame points to character. Guilt can taunt you for having been in the gutter but shame tells you that you are trash. Guilt insinuates you are disappointing but shame insists you are disgusting.

Guilt needs to be addressed and resolved before it becomes shame. Shame can cause stomach problems, insomnia, high blood pressure, and addictions. One study established that external shame — the fear that others are judging us negatively — is associated with anorexia, while internal shame — our negative self-evaluation and self-generated criticism — is associated with bulimia.[6]

Think about the way guilt and shame are used as weapons in legalistic religion. It's no wonder people are hurting! Metaphorically speaking, guilt is the imp that matures into the demon of shame who inflicts pain and afflicts people with problems that can only be resolved when they understand the full meaning of forgiveness. Live with shame long enough and it can kill you.

FORGIVENESS CURES SIN

In chapter four, we discussed the meaning of the word "sin" when we considered the interpretation of *hamartia*. Remember, the word consists of two parts: *ha*, the prefix that negates, and *martia*, derived from *meros*, which means form or identity. Together, the prefix and root of the word means "no form." So, there is a sense in which any person lives in sin who doesn't know the truth of who he is.

Then there is the plural word, "sins," which refer to the actions stemming from a false understanding of our identity. Think of sin as the root of the problem and sins as the bitter fruit. When we talk about the forgiveness of sins, many people immediately interpret the discussion through the lens of jurisprudence by seeing a divine judge who has pardoned us from crimes committed by violating his laws.

> The most common misunderstanding about Adam's disobedience is the notion that he had committed a violation against God's law that was equivalent to a crime. That is

not what happened at all. Adam's
disobedience allowed him to
become infected with the disease
(dis-ease) of sin.

He lost the ease of resting in his authentic identity and was
stricken with a horrific malady that would not only bring
death to him but was hereditary and would affect his family
for generations to come.

Was God angry? Not toward Adam. Our Loving Father's
heart is filled with compassion for those who sin. His anger
is stirred by what He sees destroy a person but not toward
the person.

Allow me to share a very personal illustration (which I have
been given permission to share). Melanie, my dear wife of
over fifty years, suffers with debilitating health issues accompanied by chronic and severe pain. There are times I have
witnessed her in agony and have felt feelings of anger rising
within me. Am I angry toward her? Absolutely not! To
suggest such a thing would be ludicrous. The anger I feel is
toward the pain and its cause.

When my wife senses or even sees my anger, she recognizes
that my emotions are an expression of my love for her. She
knows our relationship and doesn't for one moment think

the anger is toward her. She sees it for what it is — anger toward *the disease* that afflicts her. What she sees is *passion* for her wellbeing, based on deep love.

In the same way, God is not angry toward us but neither is He indifferent toward the disease of sin that harms and even destroys those He loves. As previously discussed in earlier chapters, His wrath is His passion for us, not against us. His justice aims toward the goal of restoration not revenge. He indeed loves us but hates it when we fall into sins because of what it does *to us*.

> The fundamental nature of sin isn't a damnable infraction but a deadly infection that needed and received miraculous intervention. What Adam required wasn't an angry judge but a Great Physician.

Thankfully, that is exactly what humanity received in Jesus Christ. He is the both the Physician and Cure for sin (singular) and sins (plural). The cancer of sin has met its match in Jesus. As the old hymn, "Once For All" assures us, "Jesus has died and there is remission!"

Sadly, the modern church has largely lost sight of sin as a condition pitied by God and sees it as a crime to be punished by God. May we regain the orthodox view of sin so we can move from guilt to grace!

Allow me to reference another hymn that clearly affirms the truth of the nature of sin and how Christ has fully and successfully dealt with it. It begins in 1674, when a little boy was born in Southampton, England. This child was born into a Christian family with a father who was a strong believer. In fact, his dad was jailed twice because of his commitment to allowing the Scriptures to direct his beliefs and practice instead of going along with whatever the Church of England told him he must believe. They called him a "nonconformist," and nonconformity has never been allowed in the world of religion.

This boy became a preacher at the age of twenty-four and preached for many years. But his preaching isn't what he is remembered for today. Today, he is remembered for being a hymn-writer who wrote songs many of us grew up singing. In fact, he wrote over five hundred hymns, such as "Marching to Zion," "Oh God, Our Help In Ages Past," and "When I Survey The Wondrous Cross." He also wrote the Christmas carol, "Joy to the World."

In 1707, he wrote a hymn that beautifully explains the precious solution Jesus has provided as the cure for sin. That man's name is Isaac Watts, and the hymn is called "Sin, Like A Venomous Disease." Watts correctly understood sin for what it is. Allow the impact of these lyrics to settle into your understanding.[7]

Sin, like a venomous disease,

Infects our vital blood;

The only balm is sovereign grace,

And the physician, God.

Our beauty and our strength are fled,

And we draw near to death;

But Christ the Lord recalls the dead

With his almighty breath.

Madness by nature reigns within,

The passions burn and rage,

Till God's own Son, with skill divine,

The inward fire assuage.

We lick the dust, we grasp the wind,

And solid good despise;

Such is the folly of the mind,

Till Jesus makes us wise.

We give our souls the wounds they feel,

We drink the pois'nous gall,

And rush with fury down to hell;

But Heav'n prevents the fall.

FORGIVENESS TAKES AWAY SIN

Seeing that sin isn't a crime for which we are convicted and sentenced but a hereditary organic condition that needed to be cured, we are able to better understand exactly what happened through Jesus Christ in regard to sin.

> The word "forgive" doesn't mean what many have been told. It doesn't fit inside a judicial system of judgment and punishment by God. Is there punishment for sin? Absolutely, but it is *sin that punishes*, not God. Sin brings its own consequences.

Forgiveness is a word associated with taking something away, the way chemo can take away cancer. In the Hebrew language in which the Old Testament Scriptures were written, the most common word used for "forgive" is *nasa*, which means to pick something up and carry it away.[8] One example of where the word is used is in Psalm 32:1: "Blessed is he whose transgression is *forgiven*, whose sin is covered." The word used there is *nasa*. The word can be translated in other ways too, but is translated as "forgive" in eight verses.

For instance, when Nehemiah was about to go into the King's presence, the Bible says he "took up (*nasa*) the wine and gave it to the king" (Nehemiah 2:1). When God reminded Israel of His faithfulness, He said, "You yourselves have seen what I did to the Egyptians, and how I bore (*nasa*) you on eagle's wings and brought you to Myself" (Exodus 19:4). When Jonah found himself in the boat with the others, and they were all about to die in a storm because of his sin, he said to them, "Pick me up (*nasa*) and throw me into the sea" (Jonah 1:12). The list could go on and on because the word is used 611 times in the Old Testament.

What about forgiveness in the New Testament? There are two words in the original language of the New Testament that are translated "forgive." The first is the word *aphiemi* and means to send or make go away. The word is used 133 times and is similar in usage as the Old Testament Hebrew word, *nasa*. It denotes the idea that something is taken away.

The word is used 1 John 2:12: "I am writing to you, little children, because your sins have been forgiven you for His name's sake." John was saying that through the cross sins have been taken away and the tense of the verb even indicate that the result will be an ongoing reality. It is a forgiveness that shows our sins have been forever sent away. It's not about an angry God deciding to move past His anger over our sins.

The other word used in the New Testament that is translated "forgive" is the word *charizomai*. The root of the word is *charis*, which means "grace." It is used nineteen times and denotes the action of doing something pleasant, gracious, and benevolent toward another person.[9] Divine forgiveness, then, is the gracious act of taking our sins away from us and never associating them with us again.

You may have made choices that have left you with feeling of guilt and shame but God's grace is bigger than your guilt. 1 John 3:20 says, ""Whenever our heart condemns us; for God is greater than our heart and knows all things" (NASB). *The Message* translation is even clearer in making the point. "Whenever we feel guilty, God is greater and more powerful than our conscience, and he knows everything there is to know about us."

Just believe what God says. Just believe that Jesus did no less than He came to do. John the Baptist called Him, "the Lamb of God who takes away the sins of the world" and John was right. Reject guilt and receive Grace. That's all any of us needs to do. Religion will tell you that more is needed. Asking for forgiveness? Already done. Rededicating yourself to Christ? It doesn't work and isn't necessary. Promising to try harder to do better? Don't go there — it's idolatrous because it seeks to substitute works for His finished work.

Consider the well-known story of the prodigal son. He left the pig pen fully intending to rededicate himself to his father. Would you agree with that? His plan was to go home and confess to his father that he had sinned and that, from this point on, he would serve him better. "I've sinned against heaven and in your sight and am not worthy to be your son. Make me as one of your servants" (Luke 15:21). "I've sinned, but promise to be a good servant now." Can this be called anything other than "rededication?"

However, when he got home, the father rejected his attempt at rededication. He wouldn't even give his son time to ask for forgiveness or make promises. He immediately fell on him, hugging him and celebrating his homecoming. He didn't want his son to rededicate Himself. Instead, He insisted on something greater — repentance. Repentance from what? Pig pens and far country excursions? No, repentance from rejecting his father's unconditional love and acceptance. How had he done that? By thinking that there was something he needed to do instead of simply receiving his father's love.

I believe Jesus had the father pour out his love on his son before he gave his speech to show that the father didn't want the son to make a connection between his father's acceptance and his own rededication. The bewildered son wasn't given the chance to make any promises. His only choice was to either relax in his father's arms and accept his acceptance, or pull away. The way the story unfolds shows us which choice he made.

He never did rededicate himself. Instead, he repented right there in his father's arms. Don't jump to the wrong conclusion about his repentance. I don't mean he never repented of his sins. That was imbedded in the process, but more importantly he repented of the faulty view he had held about his father. He had thought he wanted a confession. He thought he wanted commitment to do better. In reality the only thing his father wanted was Him.

This son's repentance didn't happen in the pigpen when he decided to come home. It happened in his father's embrace, when his father wrapped his arms around his son and the boy gave up his silly notions of doing a better job and decided instead to simply rest in his father's hug.

He repented of a faulty concept of who his father was, and that is what empowered him to never go back to the far country again. His decision in the pig pen to ask for forgiveness and rededicate himself was well-intentioned, but it was shallow and silly. His father's embrace brought the revelation that what he needed wasn't rededication, but repentance of the foolish concept he had held about his dad.

Have you rededicated yourself again and again? I feel your pain. I did it countless times myself. I encourage you now to stop it. Stop it permanently.

> Don't ever rededicate yourself to God again. Instead, repent. Your need is not to do a better job in a religious regiment. Repentance is a change of direction. To repent may require that your understanding of who God is and how you see Him turns one hundred eighty degrees. Our Father doesn't want our promises. He just wants us. It is when we truly know that fact, that everything changes.

You may not feel lovable, especially when you've done wrong and strayed far from the path you intended to follow. You may feel guilty or even feel shame. You may question how the Father could love you given all you know about yourself but the truth is that He does love you. His love isn't contingent on your actions, past or present. His love is unconditional, unwavering, and unending.

Understanding the love of the Father is foundational. It is the bedrock upon which everything else stands. Until we grasp this love, we can't live healthy lives because we were created to share in the Father's love. The Father, Son, and Holy Spirit have always lived in a circle of love and they want you to enjoy it too. The purpose of the Trinity in creating humanity was so that we could be included in that circle of love.

Know this: you are loved and forgiven. The pathway to understanding and accepting this loving forgiveness isn't always easy. It requires us to confront our own feelings of unworthiness and to challenge our preconceived notions about love and acceptance. But as we make this journey, we can find comfort in the fact that we are not alone. The Father is with us every step of the way, guiding us, comforting us, and loving us with an extravagant love that knows no bounds.

QUESTIONS FOR REFLECTION

1. How does understanding sin as a failure to recognize our true identity as children of God change your perspective on shame and guilt?
2. The author discusses the concept of "sonship" as a cure for shame. Share how embracing your identity as a beloved child of God has impacted your life or could impact it.
3. Reflect on a time when you felt burdened by shame or guilt. How does the book's message offer a different way of dealing with these feelings?

4. Discuss the role of the Holy Spirit in moving from a place of shame to one of sonship. How have you experienced the Spirit's work in revealing your true identity in Christ?

5. The chapter suggests that overcoming shame involves a deep realization of God's complete acceptance and forgiveness. How can this understanding transform relationships within the Christian community?

AFTERWORD

The religious composition of the United States has significantly changed over the past few decades. In the early 1990s, about 90% of U.S. adults identified as Christians, but this number has since decreased to about two-thirds. The percentage of adults who identify as atheist, agnostic, or "nothing in particular" has grown from 16% in 2007 to 29% today. The trend gained momentum in the 1990s and has continued since then.[1]

In 1972, nationwide surveys began asking Americans, "What is your religious preference?" 90% identified as Christian, and 5% were religiously unaffiliated. In the next two decades, the share of "nones" grew slowly, reaching 9% in 1993. But then disaffiliation started speeding up – in 1996, the share of unaffiliated Americans jumped to 12%, and two years later, it was 14%. This growth has continued, and 29% of Americans now say they have "no religion."

According to the General Social Survey (GSS) – an extensive, nationally representative survey with consistent data on religious affiliation going back several decades, many have switched out of the religion they were raised to become religiously unaffiliated. Some identify as "nones," but others identify as "dones." They're done with it all.[2]

I recognize it's controversial for me to say this, but I understand and can even appreciate it in some instances. The vision of God presented in many churches today is disgraceful in the truest sense of the word. The Abba of Jesus has been evicted from legalistic churches and replaced with a god who looks nothing like the One revealed in Jesus Christ. It's not surprising that people finally grow weary enough of that idolatrous image to walk away from it.

I have written this book with two aims in mind. The first was to influence a change in the way some readers have seen God until now. If your concept of God doesn't look like Jesus Christ, you've accepted a substitute. Jesus alone is the "exact representation" (Hebrews 1:3) of who God is. If it doesn't look like Him, it's not his Father. My main goal is that we would all understand how everything about Him can be understood through His love. If this book has changed the way you see Him, my mission has been accomplished. Even if it has caused you to rethink some of the things you've believed until now, I'm grateful for that, too.

The second reason I wrote this book was to guide readers toward seeing themselves differently. We've been told so much for so long that has been so wrong about who we are. I know because I was guilty of doing it myself when I was a pastor for over twenty years. I hope you see that you are more than legalistic religion has told you. I pray that your identity in Christ will be the North Star that guides you because any false identity put on you by misguided religious messages will mislead you.

So, that's the end game of this book: To change how you see God and yourself. Those two transformative steps are the pathway back to New Testament Christianity.

If you want to know more about this and other relevant subjects, you can find me on Facebook and YouTube. You may also be interested in an online subscription group I teach daily. In that community, we discuss practical ways to express grace in many areas of life. The teachings are available to watch at the viewers' convenience. It's a great group of people from diverse walks of life. We would be happy to have you join us. You can get information about this community and see the topics we have studied at www.-gracewalkexperience.com.

Thank you for investing your time in this book. May the Spirit of Truth guide you into an ever-expanding knowledge of Life.

NOTES

2. FROM REVENGE TO RESTORATION

1. Walter A. Bordenn, "A History of Justice: Origins of Law and Psychiatry," APPL Newsletter, vol. 24, no. 2, April 1999. Available online at the time of printing at www.aapi.org/newsletter/N242hist_justice.htm
2. The reality of divine justice does not nullify the need for human justice in this world. This chapter doesn't suggest that grace exempts those who do wrong from societal correction. Romans 13:1-7 is clear that governments are ordained by God and serve a role in promoting good conduct and punishing wrongdoing. That, however, is another subject. This chapter addresses divine justice without denying the proper place for judicial justice executed by God-ordained civil authority. Nor does this chapter imply that sinful behavior won't bring its own consequences
3. https://www.prisonfellowship.org/2021/07/joe-amy-story-reconciliation/

3. FROM PUNISHMENT TO PASSION

1. There are two Greek words for wrath in the New Testament. The less commonly used word, *thumos*, is associated with anger. It is used in the New Testament eighteen times, ten of those times being in the book of Revelation, where the word is used in reference to the "wrath of God" seven times. (See Revelation 14:10, 14:19, 15:1, 15:7, 16:1, 16:19, 19:15) Is God's anger in the apocalyptic use of the word in Revelation disassociated from His love? It can't be because God's nature is love and will always be love. Out of the eighteen times the word "wrath" is used in a way that denotes anger, it is used seven times in a book of the Bible that warrants much study before we conclude that God is mad at those who don't love Him. There is hardly enough evidence in the book of Revelation to justify the kind of widespread view that pollutes the religious world today, one of an angry deity whose fury can only be satisfied by payback. God's anger can be directed toward sin but not those infected by sin. If a loved

one has cancer, you may feel anger toward that disease but not the one you love.

2. *Strong's Concordance* #3709 states the definition as: 1. Anger, the natural disposition, temper, character. 2. Movement or agitation of the soul, impulse, desire, any violent emotion.

3. Augustine, *City of God*, book 30, chap. 17.

4. Reference to the author's book, *Beyond an Angry God*, and the specific chapter, "Not Your Grandmother's Hell."

5. Thomas Merton, *New Seeds of Contemplation*, (New York: New Directions, 2007), pp. 123-124.

6. Alexandre Kalomiros, *The River of Fire*, (Seattle: Saint Nectarios Press, 1980), p. 35.

4. FROM SINNERS TO SAINTS

1. Steve McVey, *Grace Walk*, (Harvest House Publishers, 1995).

2. Francois Du Toit, *The Mirror Bible*, (MirrorWord Publishing, 2023).

3. *Strong's Concordance, Entry #1391.* Original word is δόξα, ης, ἡ. Part of Speech: Noun, Feminine. Phonetic Spelling: (dox'-ah) Definition: opinion (always good in NT), praise, honor, glory.

4. I'm thinking of how an animal is sometimes hobbled to restrict its ability to move freely, typically by tying its legs together or attaching a device that limits its range of motion. Historically, cruel owners have sometimes even broken the leg of the animal.

5. Colossians 1:27 says that Christ is in you. In John 14:17, Jesus told His disciples that the Spirit "lives with you and will be in you." Ephesians 3:16-17 says that His Spirit is in your inner being. 1 Corinthians 3:16 says that God's Spirit dwells in you. 2 Timothy 1:14 says that the Holy Spirit lives in us. You can use Google to search the Bible and find it repeatedly teaches that the Spirit of Christ is in you and defines you. To define ourselves in any other way is to deny the plain teaching of Scripture.

5. FROM MORAL LIVING TO MIRACULOUS LIVING

1. Steve McVey, *The Secret of Grace*, (Harvest House Publishers, Kindle Edition, pp. 64-66). Story retold with different application.

2. My point here isn't to make a case for whether Adam should be understood as a historical individual or as a metaphor representing

humanity as a whole. Either way you approach it, the lesson is the same.

6. From Guilt to Grace

1. https://www.princeton.edu/news/2013/10/08/weighed-down-guilt-research-shows-its-more-metaphor
2. *ibid*
3. I used to think legalism infects mostly conservative churches until I attended a more liberal liturgical church and heard a parish rector say, "There are three weeks left in the Lenten Season. That's twenty-one days for you to confess your sins and get your act together." It triggered memories of how I had talked the same way in the conservative world where I had served as pastor. Legalism is a pandemic across the full range of Christendom, from the far left to the far right.
4. https://psycnet.apa.org/record/2012-25093-001
5. https://pubmed.ncbi.nlm.nih.gov/19186924/
6. Troop, N. A., Allan, S., Serpell, L., & Treasure, J. L. (2008). Shame in women with a history of eating disorders. European Eating Disorders Review, 16(6), 480–488.
7. Watts, Isaac. "Sin, Like a Venomous Disease." 1707. Public domain.
8. www.biblestudytools.com/lexicons/hebrew/nas/nasa.html
9. www.biblestudytools.com/lexicons/greek/nas/charizomai.html

Afterword

1. https://www.pewresearch.org/religion/2022/09/13/how-u-s-religious-composition-has-changed-in-recent-decades/
2. https://www.pewresearch.org/religion/2024/01/24/religious-nones-in-america-who-they-are-and-what-they-believe/

About the Author

Dr. Steve McVey is the author of twenty-three books, including the best seller, *Grace Walk*. Steve writes to address specific needs in the reader's life. His books are filled with biblical truth, practical application, humor and affirmation that will encourage you and strengthen you in your own journey of faith.

Steve and his wife, Melanie, live in the Tampa Bay area of Florida. They have four adult children and five grandchildren.

Endorsements

Sixteen Grammy Award Winning Gospel Singer, Kirk Franklin said, "Steve McVey's books have been used by God to transform my Christian walk."

Fourteen Grammy Award winner, Ron Block wrote, "Steve McVey is one of the voices unafraid to tell the whole truth about grace. Steve's biblical, solid, and lifechanging writing points me to the freely-given love, favor, and grace of God in Christ - a grace walk experience."

Dr. Tony Evans, President of The Urban Alternative wrote, "My good friend, Steve McVey, has put the amazing back into grace."

Gary Smalley, author of *The Language of Love*: "Few people have had the life change effect on my life that Steve McVey has had. Whenever I hear that he has a new book, I buy several copies."

Neil Anderson, author of *The Bondage Breaker*: "*A Divine Invitation* (by Steve McVey) will enlarge your heart and increase your comprehension of God's love that goes beyond knowledge."

The late Bill Bright, Founder of Campus Crusade for Christ, wrote: "Steve McVey has given us in very clear and understandable language a wonderful, indelible picture of just how beautiful, complete and even startling God's love for us really is."

OTHER BOOKS BY STEVE MCVEY

Grace Walk

The Secret of Grace

Grace Amazing

52 Lies Heard in Church Every Sunday

Grace Walk Devotional

Helping Other Overcome Addictions (with Mike Quarles)

Unlock Your Bible

A Divine Invitation

Walking in the Will of God

When Wives Walk in Grace

The Godward Gaze

Grace Walk Moments

Getting Past the Hurt (with Melanie McVey)

The Grace Walk Experience Workbook

Journey into Intimacy Workbook

Anchored: Five Keys to a Secure Faith

Beyond an Angry God

Quantum Life

Quantum Faith

Butterfly Kisses (children's book)

Quantum Prayer

Grace in the Marketplace

Made in the USA
Coppell, TX
07 April 2024

31032818R00074